Amen!
Until Tomorrow
Retaking the Pacific After Pearl Harbor
By John D. Wolf

Fairway Press
Lima, Ohio

AMEN! UNTIL TOMORROW:
RETAKING THE PACIFIC AFTER PEARL HARBOR

FIRST EDITION
Copyright © 1990 by
John D. Wolf

CIP 90-084038

7734 / ISBN 1-55673-226-0   PRINTED IN U.S.A.

Dedication

This book is dedicated to the officers and crew of the

U.S.S. FREDERICK FUNSTON [APA 89]

and to all Marines, Soldiers, Navy C.B.s
who were landed by her boats in the battles of

Sicily
Salerno
Saipan
Guam
Leyte Gulf, P.I.
Lingayen Gulf, P.I.
Iwo Jima

Table of Contents

Foreword

Several thousand clergymen served in World War II in all branches of service. They came from all denominations. All were volunteers since clergy and seminary students were exempt from the draft. Some of the latter were pacifists who refused to register in the draft and served time in prison. Others, like myself, struggled with the war system in the light of the Scriptures, made a decision that the "war was the lesser of two evils" and decided to join our generation in the conflict. Reinhold Niebuhr played a part in that decision.

The Navy preferred chaplains directly out of seminary. While several of our classmates went to Danbury Prison, five of us enlisted from Union Theological Seminary, New York, and went to Norfolk, Virginia, for training in June 1942. At twenty-three, I was told at Chaplains' School that I was the youngest chaplain in the Navy. After initiation at Newport, Rhode Island, Training Station, where I edited the "Newport Recruit," I was ordered to the U.S.S. Frederick Funston (APA 89). I was her first chaplain and the Funston was one of the first ships converted to amphibious warfare. She was built for army transport in 1942 and made trips to the Solomon Islands. The Funston was then converted to an "attack transport" and commissioned in the navy April 24, 1943. Captain John E. Murphy, USN, was her first commanding officer.

In the beginning of the War, amphibious warfare had to be developed. Little was known on how to handle large davits, LCVPs (landing craft vehicle personnel), and LCTs (landing craft tanks), and the launching of hundreds of troops in coordination with LSTs and other newly developed vessels designed to "hit the beaches."

The Funston participated in the Sicily landings where high seas caused more damage than the enemy, and landings at Salerno, Italy, where enemy intelligence had prepared an overly warm welcome. The famous 100th Battalion, 34th Division of Japanese-Americans, was landed at Salerno. Returning from the Mediterranean with the 82nd Airborne Division, we stopped at Belfast, Ireland, leaving the 82nd and all our landing craft for the forthcoming Normandy landings. Then, through a Christmas hurricane, back to Hoboken in order to re-outfit for the Pacific war.

The role of the Funston in the Pacific was to be the "veteran attack transport" (together with her sister ship, the USS James O'Hara APA 90) in the strategy, based from Pearl Harbor, to island-hop on the way to the Philippines and eventually Tokyo. Our story begins with these battles.

A ship's chaplain serves all faiths. He conducts regular services of worship. If possible, he arranges Protestant services, Catholic mass, and Jewish services by exchanging when ships are in port. His duties will vary with conditions but always it is to look after the spiritual welfare of the men. Often he serves as counselor (navy parlance calls this "sympathy chits" or "crying towels"), librarian, recreation officer, morale officer and consultant in personnel matters. During battle stations, he worked jointly with the medical staff in meeting and tending the wounded. On the Funston we carried a surplus of doctors and corpsmen. Immediately upon landing assault troops we received casualties from the beaches — sometimes the same men we had landed.

With the cooperation of Captain Murphy and, after Saipan, Captain C.C. Anderson, USN, the Funston chaplain developed a unique and, as far as is known, the only type of lecture-messages found in this book. It became my duty and privilege to research, write and deliver these talks each evening while the ship was at evening General Quarters. (Most attacks from the enemy seemed to come at dawn and sunset). For the purposes of the messages I was allowed access to classified information.

To get the picture, imagine the ship's crew at battle stations, hundreds of Marines, soldiers or C.B.s filling every available space, listening to descriptions of activities aboard ship and in the fleet, classified information about the target island, and additional researched material about the area and the target, gleaned from the library. The response was so gratifying the captain requested the same communication not only for Saipan but for campaigns at Guam, Leyte and Lingayen Gulfs in the Philippines, and Iwo Jima. To thousands of men the Funston became affectionately known as the "Fighting Freddie."

Occasions of initiation from lowly "pollywogs" to "shellbacks" upon crossing the equator, depicted a happy ship that could play hard as well as fight hard and I might add, pray hard. Services of baptisms and Holy Communion and many burials at sea affirmed the religious faith of the servicemen. I have seen them at their worst and at their best as they met life and death in warfare.

I am appreciative of the Navy allowing me to serve twenty months on sea duty in six major battles. Later, I was assigned to serve on the faculty of the Navy Chaplain's School in Williamsburg, Virginia, and to share my experiences with incoming chaplains.

The dramatic experience of the death of the "skipper's" only son, Sgt. Charles Carter Anderson, Jr. USMC, at Iwo Jima on his father's ship was so unusual as to merit mention in *Time* magazine. "The Anderson Story" is told in a separate section.

John D. Wolf

Acknowledgements

To undertake an adventure in book publication requires the advice and encouragement of family and many friends. In particular I am grateful for my wife Carolyn and sons John Jr., Carter Anderson, and Earl Kelsey. Other relatives who served in the Navy, my brother J. Grove Wolf, cousin Arthur Wolf, and brother-in-law Dean H. Kelsey.

Former shipmates on the *Funston*, Charles A. Beasley who named a son after his chaplain, Robert L. Maxfield, and Marine Chaplain James Butler.

Friends Keith Reinert, Ralph Joseph, Richard Hamilton, Jerry Knarr, Dr. Karl Lutze of Valparaiso University, Rosemary Risk, Stanley Needham Jr., Jeanne and Guinevere Anderson-Greist, James H. Steele, and Capt. Kenneth L. Geitz, USN (Ret).

Special note should be given to Barbara Pearson who typed the manuscript and to my business advisor, Robert Klopfenstein who designed the maps. Also to Yeoman R. L. Carter who typed the original manuscript aboard the *Funston*.

The cover design was created by Earl Kelsey Wolf, naturalist and graphic designer for the Michigan Department of Natural Resources at Hoffmaster State Park, Muskegon, Michigan.

Saipan

A compilation of broadcasts to ship's personnel and troops on board U.S.S. Frederick Funston (APA-89)

Saipan

Good evening shipmates! It seems the fates of war have suddenly decreed that you, and you, and you; you Marines, C.B.'s and sailors should be shipmates; following a course set by Horace Greeley long ago with the words, "Go west young man, go west"; and expecting to do battle with the enemy at a date not too far distant. As we move nearer and nearer to "D" day we will find ourselves sharing common experiences; wondering together what various signals, lights and maneuvers may be. Few in this company of ours are not veterans of one or more campaigns. We know what to expect and yet we will share the same dilemma in having little information to go on.

Before the invasion of Sicily Adm. Alan G. Kirk said:

> *Only one out of ten men on a modern ship in combat can see what is going on. Someone must see for them. After all, this is a democratic war, and I believe that men who are willing to give their lives for democracy have the right to be included in what's going on.*

It is with this in mind that our "skipper", Captain Murphy, has endorsed a regular evening broadcast to you during general quarters. Also in time of combat the action will be reported from the bridge as accurately as possible.

In this broadcast your roving reporter or chief scuttle-butter hopes to bring the ship and convoy news that you want to hear. At the end there will be a brief resume of the latest world news.

Flash! Now here is the big scoop of the day we have been waiting for. We are now on our way to Eniwetok, in the Marshall Islands. This is our staging area. It will take us ten days to reach this atoll where some troops will be transferred to LST's. After two days at the staging area we will get underway for the target. And where is the target? Well, you can't expect all the news in one night.

11

Tomorrow's broadcast will concern this mighty convoy which you have curiously watched gather today, as we say, foregathered. Watch it form! It is part of the greatest naval armada the world has ever seen. But more of that tomorrow.

Just one word of warning. Up to this time you could be pretty careless about what went over the side. We realize that when the sea is rough you can't help "riding the rail". But don't feed the fishes cigarette butts, paper, cans or 'what-have-you'. Perhaps you have never heard of Willy and his brothers. Willy is known to most destroyer and sub-chaser men as a particularly canny underwater dog with an acute sense of smell. He hangs around outside the islands and reports to Tokyo what goes on. Unfortunately he has never been sunk. Don't make it easy for Willy! In a convoy this size he could follow us all the way to Tokyo if everyone threw their empty cigarette packages overboard.

Amen! until tomorrow.

The Jig-Saw Puzzle   May 31, 1944

This has been a quiet day. If you were reminded of the song "Smoke gets in my eyes", or perhaps dear old Pittsburgh this afternoon, it is because smoke is going to play an important part in hiding us from enemy planes and incidentally in keeping us from seeing what is going on. As we have enjoyed the restfulness of a sapphire sea punctured by the graceful flying fish or the beautiful phosphorus glow of last night, it is hard for us to realize the real purpose of our mission. Yet the evidence is all around us and perhaps you will be interested in how this little piece of the jig-saw puzzle, our ships, fits into the total plan.

In our convoy are twenty-two ships and about twelve escorts. Broken down it consists of twelve amphibious transports like the *Funston*, six cargo ships, two LSD's and two escort carriers. Included among the escorts are five or six destroyers, three destroyer transports, and three minesweepers.

Dead ahead of us is the *Monrovia* with Commodore Knowles, divisional and group commander of transport group 18, aboard. Ahead of the *Monrovia* is the *Cambria* with our direct boss and second in command, Rear Adm. Hill, aboard. On the port side in order is the *Bolivar*, *Sheridan*, *Comet*, *Doyen*, etc. To starboard is the *Clay*, *Middleton*, *Neville*, *Feland*, etc. The carriers with their welcome planes are generally in the rear.

Perhaps you have noticed that the convoy keeps 600 yards between ships in the columns and 1,000 yards between columns. It is of the utmost importance to keep in formation, as you can imagine, not only because of the possibilities of collision but because our escort protection is organized on the basis of our keeping position. If one ship gets out of line it therefore endangers the entire convoy. In a way it is like a football player getting offside and thereby penalizing his whole team.

Even though we can only see thirty-four pieces in this gigantic puzzle, don't fool yourself into thinking this is what I meant when I said this operation "is to be the greatest amphibious operation in naval history." You will never see it all. To imagine eighteen battleships, fifty carriers and a proportional number of cruisers and destroyers, plus all the auxiliary transports, cargoes, LSD's, LST's, LCI's, etc. would be like trying to imagine the national debt. After all this division of ships is carrying little more than part of the 2nd Marine Division. Other divisions in the northern task force are carrying the entire 4th Division and the 27th Army Division. The LST's are carrying the balance of the assault troops. Then there is the southern task force carrying the 3rd Marines and the 1st Provisional Marine Brigade. All is under the command of the famous Vice-Adm. Kelly Turner, strong right arm of Adm. Nimitz. Adm. Turner is aboard the *Rocky Mount*.

Could it be that you have failed to notice another historic feature of our expedition. For the first time, a large scale amphibious operation is to be All-American. American led from the top down, American planned with ample room for American initiative in the pinches, American ships and American troops. Which brings me to a bit of American humor that was overheard topside today. A Marine remarked to a sailor somewhat sarcastically, "I hear the place we are going to take has two towns. The Navy is going to bombard one and save the other for liberty."

For you amateur navigators to check your computations, here are a few figures. We are headed in a west-south-west direction at an average speed of 13 knots. At 1800 we were approximately 2,000 miles from Eniwetok and approximately 300 miles from Pearl Harbor.

Amen! until tomorrow.

In The Know   **June 1, 1944**

The scuttlebutt tonight is hot. You are really going to be in the "know" from now on. First is the big news from near at home. Hang on to your lifeboats! At about 1000 today two erratic torpedoes were fired at one of our carriers. Obviously fired by Willy and his buddies, one was definitely sighted and the wake of the other was also seen. The "fish" were evidently fired from some distance because they appeared to be nearly "spent" when sighted. In other words it looked like a "shoot and pray" affair and we can thank God tonight that he turned a deaf ear to Willy's petition. In any event this news should shake the last atom of carelessness out of our system. Shades of the destroyer *Bristol* leaped to our memories; of how she was with our Mediterranean convoy at evening general quarters and was gone at dawn. Willy threw two slow balls. The next one may be over the middle of the plate. All the odds are on our side. We've been warned. Let's be alert!

Add to this scoop the confirmation of our objective. Somewhere on this ship I am sure there is at least one, one lonely man, who does not know what the target is. Two days ago I could have said Flash. Now all I can say is fizzle. But for the benefit of that lonely man who is not "in the know", I say, *Flash*. Our target is the island of Saipan, in the Mariana Islands. In following broadcasts you will be told more and more about the objective and our part in taking it. Briefly, I can describe Saipan as 1,121 miles from Eniwetok and about 1,500 miles from Tokyo and Manila. It is the most important of the southern group of the Marianas which also consist of Tinian, Rota and Guam, all of which will be taken in due time.

In appearance the island has a resemblance to a kangaroo sitting on its haunches. If you accept this resemblance it is easy for me to point out that we intend to kick him right in the _____ ; well you know. Check the maps in the library and forward Recreation Room and I'll tell you more tomorrow.

In case during an abandon ship drill the Bos'n. mate forgets to say "simulate" in step three, the following information will be of value. Tonight we will be 100 miles from Johnston Island off our starboard beam. This was the furthest outpost of the U.S. Navy air force before we gained other bases in the Marshalls. We are 670 miles from Pearl Harbor, 1,900 from Eniwetok.

Some of you publicity-mongers have asked what coverage the press will give to this campaign. Here is the dope. Scattered throughout the various task forces are 230 correspondents, photographers and observers. You don't need to worry, even the folks in Eyewash, Mississippi, will hear the "shot that goes round the world." Aboard our own ship we have Larry MacManus, feature writer and Bill Young, photographer, both of Yank, the armed service's weekly. Bill has already taken candid shots in the Aleutians and the Marshalls and Larry wore out several pencils at Makin Island. We also have several observers with us who will become known to you later.

Perhaps some of you have heard talk emanating from Washington that the Army, Navy and Air Force would be united into one department. Our able troop commander, Lt. Col. Miller, says this is impossible. Why? Well, naturally, because there are not enough Marine uniforms to go around.

Some others seem lost in regard to the time, or the date or even the year. To help you out a bit; it is now 1842 the first day of June, in the year of our Lord 1944.

Amen! until tomorrow.

Let's Get Acquainted   June 6, 1944

While you are still trying to pronounce those two new names that have suddenly been lifted off the map and placed in your vocabulary, I'll try and tell you something about the most important one tonight. My authority is nothing more than two little pamphlets put out by Naval Intelligence and the 2nd Marine Division plus an article in National Geographic of June 1942 by William Price, later published in book form under the title, "Japan's Hidden Islands".

SaEEban, or just plain Saipan if you leave the belch out, is one of the Marianas. In 1521 no other personage than Magellan himself sighted the islands and gave them the poetic name Isles of the Lateen Sails. After he entered the port of Guam and had been pretty thoroughly looted by the swarming natives, he crossed the fancy name off his logbook and substituted Ladrones, meaning Thieves.

For more than a century they were so known. Spanish priests then settled on the islands and named them after the widow of the Spanish king, Maria Anna. On several occasions either England or America might have had the islands. For example, in the Spanish-American war the cruiser *Charlestown* entered Guam's harbor and fired at the antiquated Spanish fort. Instead of a similar reply, out came a boat of Spanish officials. When they climbed aboard they apologized for not answering what they supposed to be a salute. They explained they had no powder. Imagine their surprise when they were told the U.S. and Spain were at war. After the war we retained only Guam and the Philippines, returning the rest of the islands of Micronesia to Spain. What did Spain do then but turn around and sell these islands to Germany for $4,500,000.

16

Somehow it seems that history has a way of punishing us for our lack of foresight. No sooner had World War I begun but Japan seized all German islands in the name of the Allies. For this noble contribution to the Allied cause she paid the price of 300 killed and a few hundred more casualties. From that time on these islands have been like a two-edged axe, one cutting edge facing Hawaii and the other deep in the Philippines. The handle, of course, is swung by Tokyo. The result has been evident.

We have chosen to strike at the most important of these islands. Saipan is the center of the Japanese civilian government for all the Marianas. It is the main military and supply base. Since 1914 no foreign ships have been allowed near it and practically no American civilians. Most of the information that I will pass on to you therefore has been gained through naval intelligence, aerial and submarine photographs, etc. Let's take a look at the general features of our objective.

I said last night it resembled a kangaroo. Down the center of the island is a chain of mountains like a spinal cord. Highest of these mountains is volcanic Topotchau, 1,554 feet high. The coast has little resemblance to Waikiki, being mostly cliffs, which remind us of the volcanic origin of the island. On the west or back, are a number of impressing reefs. One around the main town of Garapan and extending down to near the foot, past the second town of Charan-Kanoa. This is the side we will strike.

On the east or front side is a beautiful bay called Magicienne Bay. This pouch looks very inviting for landing operations, but like many another beautiful and alluring creatures, it is only deceiving. It is a fortress.

Tonight there is no scoop. We are 954 miles from Eniwetok and 1,627 miles from Pearl Harbor. Which may be why an anonymous donor has made an offer to us. Since we are all in a vague philosophical mood anyway he will give a carton of cigarettes for the best poem and another for the best short story (not over 500 words). All you amateur Bobby Burns and John Steinbecks will have until Monday night to turn them in. I almost forgot to mention, they have to be original.

Amen! until tomorrow.

Rescue And Enigma   June 3, 1944

This morning a dramatic story took place on the sea right under the eyes of the convoy. It is a story marked by alertness, tragedy, and a humanitarianism of which all Americans are proud. In detail it happened like this. At 0700 the carrier escort *White Plains* reported a man overboard while on course. Immediately the alarm was given and a rubber raft thrown to him. A few moments later the destroyer *Porterfield* had sighted the man and picked him up. Said the *White Plains* to the *Porterfield*, "Thank you for your good work!"

As if this was not enough for one day, at 0930 the same carrier reported a plane overboard. An alert destroyer, the *Callaghan*, rushed to the scene and picked up the pilot. Some pessimist once said, "Bad news comes in threes." Yes, it happened again. Another plane crashed ahead of the *Callaghan* shortly thereafter, or at the same time. The pilot was again picked up but the second occupant of the plane was given up for lost after a search. At divine services tomorrow morning, this unknown flyer, who is the first casualty thus far in this campaign, will be given special remembrance.

It is always gratifying to us to note the concern taken by such a large military organization as the Navy for the individual. I often wonder what would happen if a man fell overboard from a German or Japanese warship in war time? Would everything be done to save him, even at such risk to the convoy? A few weeks hence we may not be able to show such consideration for the individual. It is however, a renewal of our faith in democracy that the little man should be of such importance under such circumstances.

18

Well, we are steaming right along. When these carrier planes flash by it makes us think of the fable of the tortoise and the hare. Nevertheless, at 2200 tonight our little 13 knots has brought us half-way, exactly 1,290 miles from Eniwetok and Pearl Harbor. Of even greater interest for us is to know that tomorrow at about 1400 we will cross that mysterious enigma, the International Date Line. The conscientious man has been unnecessarily worried about this freak. He may think he will stand an extra watch, or lose a day's pay. As the angels said, "Fear not"! What you may be able to do however, is hit the sack at 1345, awake a half hour later to discover that you have slept 24½ hours. Or you can go up to a shipmate and say, "Bet you five bucks you don't know what day this is." Not being wised-up he will say it is Sunday because he suddenly saw an officer with his tie on. By the time you are through arguing it will be Monday and you win. It is just as simple as that.

For those of you who want to dig deeper into the subject I can explain it this way. The globe is like a barrel with twenty-four staves or zones in it. Each zone represents one hour. Taking Greenwich as a starting point and traveling west you lose an hour in each zone. You can see this cannot continue indefinitely. The time must be made up somehow. So to balance off the loss with a gain, an international date line was set way out here at the 180th Meridian where it would interfere with the least number of people. When you are notified of the change you will not set your watches, just pull off another day on the calendar, put it in your pocket until you go home someday, because when you go east you will have to put it back. Is that clear? You might be interested to know that every navigator has a dream that someday he will cross the equator and the international date line at the same time.

If you happened to be on the boat deck during the midwatch last night you might have noticed two officers vigorously trying to remove the girdle of flesh that has been competing with their lifebelts for prominence. This isn't a bad example for all of us. We have had little exercise in the past three weeks and therefore must get into shape for "D" day fast. For this purpose cargo climbing nets have been rigged over the after kingposts and a boxing ring on top number four hatch. Use these at every opportunity. There is also a horizontal bar on the boat deck. But all this is not sufficient unless you are willing every day to take half an hour and work out. All you need is a space two by six to get into fighting trim.

Last night a Marine was vigorously shaken awake by one of his buddies. "What is it? Another torpedo?" he said, as he grabbed his lifebelt. "Hell no, the ice cream parlor is open." It was really good wasn't it?

Amen! until tomorrow.

The Other War   June 5, 1944

Good evening Trusty Dragon Backs:

"Having crossed the 180th Meridian on the U.S.S. *Frederick Funston*, 1300, 4 June 1944, Latitude $10^{\circ}30$'', and having been initiated then and there into the Oriental Mysteries of the Honorable Ancestors of the Golden Dragon, you are and will be recognized as a Trusty Dragon Back. By order of Golden Dragons; Ruler of 180th Meridian." Fortunately we were all made members without the initiation usually required.

Tonight we have a scoop that forces me to reverse our usual procedure. From our world news comes a FLASH FROM THE FIFTH ARMY IN ROME: Troops of Gen. Mark Clark's Fifth Army have completed the occupation of Rome, the first Axis fortress to fall under the domination of the allied army. Correspondents with the Fifth Army report in dispatches sent out from the Eternal City that the mopping up of German resistance was complete at 3:01 p.m. (N.Y. time). The Fifth Army now has complete control of the heart of the city and all outskirts. It is understood that a few snipers are still active in the eastern outskirts.

And now to nearer our floating home. At 1015 last night the destroyer *Cony* reported a sub contact on their port quarter (which would be off our starboard quarter). The *Cony* dropped four depth charges. At 2235 the destroyer *Callaghan*, one of the carrier escorts prominent in yesterday's news, reported sighting a torpedo wake passing from starboard to port. Of lesser importance is the news that the *Warhawk* developed some steering difficulties and dropped to a position at the rear of this column.

And here is a little more knowledge about Saipan to add to our growing acquaintance with that little-known fly-speck of the Pacific. Perhaps you have wondered what its people are like since it is because of them that we are out here. The natives themselves constitute only a small number of the whole. Originally they migrated as a pure Polynesian race from the Malay Archipelago. There is evidence on the islands of a very high standard of culture in this period before the time of Christ. But being so close to China, Japan, the Philippines and East Indies, bloods were gradually mixed until a melting-pot mixture, speaking a jig-saw puzzle of tongues, resulted. They are called Chamorros and Kanakas. Fifteen years of German rule made little difference except to teach some of the oldsters to say "Guten morgen." But under thirty years of Japanese rule the islands have been colonized by Koreans and Japanese until they outnumber the natives 10-1.

Economically all of these islands, except Guam, depend on sugar cane. As in Hawaii there are plantations where the cane is planted, harvested, hauled into one end of the mills and comes out sugar at the other end. Also grown are tropical fruits, yams, taro and fresh vegetables. Fish is plentiful and there is some wild game. But it is the chief exportation, sugar, that dominates the island. It is for this work that new labor had to be imported. Sugar is the cause of the sweet smell that not only hangs over the big roaring factory at Charan-Kanoa but pervades the whole island, and seems to have attracted all the flies of the Pacific.

It might interest you to know that the Japanese are not the only pests on Saipan. The fly is not without honor there. One author tells the story of going into a wayside fruit shop for lunch and having to fight the flies for every bite. The Japanese policeman ordered bean soup. When it was set before him it contained six flies. He watched with curiosity. Would he send it back? Would he pick out the flies with his chopsticks?

He raised the bowl to his mouth, locked his long upper teeth over the edge to form a sieve, and drank the soup. The six flies remained in the bowl. He smiled, "We get used to them," he said.

These sugar people never kill flies because a certain species feed on the larvae of sugar cane pests. Because it is difficult to distinguish varieties, all flies gain immunity. So, they claim, a fly saved the island. We hope it will be as easy for us to take over.

From flies to poems is quite a jump. All poems and short stories are due tomorrow night by 2200. They can be left at the Chaplain's Office or the library desk. In answer to inquiries; there is no limit to the subject matter and no one is barred from entry. Already a considerable number has been turned in so the competition will be keen. From the Marine Corps, Capt. Skinner and Capt. Koffer will be judges and from the ship, Dr. Bryer, Lt. (jg) Creighton, and Lt. (jg) Dunn.

And here is the special story for tonight. We have a new name for the Promenade decks. A Marine officer called the bridge and referred to the promenade deck as the "Marmalade deck."

Amen! until tomorrow.

We Infiltrate   June 6, 1944

Good evening shipmates.

Most of us were glad for a few incidents to break the monotony of a hot and uneventful day. You may have some mail

22

delivered by pony express, automobile, motorcycle or airplane and now you can say you saw it arrive by minesweeper. The U.S.S. *Herald* took a line off the starboard quarter and transferred special guard mail to the ship from the Admiral. For this purpose she used a 3" shell container.

The only other incident to report was the sighting of a mysterious light by the *Callaghan* at 0937. Shortly thereafter the light was reported to be friendly but we are still in the dark regarding any details.

If you were to superimpose a map of the United States over the area we have traveled and have the coast of Maine touch Pearl Harbor you would find us now around central Kansas. Perhaps some of you have become aware that we are only a few hundred miles from the nearest Marshall Islands and 800 miles from Eniwetok. It is now clear that we will go through the Marshalls. Our course will change to due west tonight. Therefore you will want to know something about them.

Like the Marianas, the Marshalls have also been in Japanese hands for thirty years. It was from here that the attack of December 7, 1941, upon Pearl Harbor was probably launched. It was here that our Navy first struck back in its brilliant raid on February 1, 1942, surprising fleets of seacraft and aircraft at Kwajalein, Wotje, Maloelap and Jaluit. Past this point American convoys have sailed for northern Australia and have been attacked by aircraft from these atolls. They are the outer edge of the great two-edged axe.

Japanese bases still exist on four of the smaller atolls of the nearer Ratak Chain. Those are Wotje, Maloelap, Mili and Jaluit. (Incidentally the definition of that now familiar word "atoll" is: a ring-shaped coral island nearly or quite enclosing a lagoon). These atoll bases have been constantly plastered by our bombers and fighters and they are no longer able to obtain food or supplies. The atolls are not self-sufficient and with the war moving around and past them, they may be ready to surrender or commit hari-kari at any time.

The enemy has learned that there are different ways to use the technique of infiltration. From January 31 to February 6,

1944, we did that very thing when we attacked and captured Kwajalein, thus cutting off their supply line to Japan. On February 17 the 22nd Marine Regiment of the 1st Prov. Brigade under Brig. Gen. Watson, and the 106th Regiment of the Army's 27th Division, captured Eniwetok on the inner ring of the Marshalls. Gen. Watson is now a Major Gen. and in command of the 2nd Marine Division. It is expected that these units will join us there.

On the whole, the Marshalls are picturesque coral atolls made up of about thirty different groups. From ten miles out we will be able to see the coconut palms and breadfruit trees on the larger islands. The smaller islands are barren. Japanese government headquarters are on Jaluit and ten years ago reported the population as 10,000. The natives are all Kanakas and bear some resemblance to native Hawaiians. They are generally idle and dislike working though some are skilled in handling and building small ships. The stable food is copra, breadfruit and rice with fish and fowl also available.

At one time the reefs may have encircled volcanic islands that have long since submerged or worn away. Now nothing remains inside these atolls but a calm lagoon. Certain of these lagoons, like Eniwetok, measure more than thirty miles in diameter. They thus make ideal bases for naval concentrations.

Eniwetok is the largest island of the Brown atoll group. The island itself is sandy and not suitable for cultivation. In 1930 it had a population of 121. It has many flies and the water is poor, but drinkable. The connecting reefs make it appear as a huge coral. To the south is a wide passage and on the east a deep channel. These are practically the only openings.

All poems and short stories are due at 2200 tonight.

Amen! until tomorrow.

D-Day In Normandy   June 7, 1944

Good evening shipmates.

FLASH! General Eisenhower's headquarters has just announced Allied landings on the coast of northern France this morning.

You are all anxious to hear all the details possible since the initial announcement of the invasion that came over the radio this afternoon. The first word read as follows: "Under command of Gen. Eisenhower, Allied Naval Forces supported by strong air forces, began landing Allied armies this morning on the northern coast of France. Gen. Montgomery is in command of Allied armies carrying out the assault.

In a special order of the day to all soldiers, sailors and airmen under his command Gen. Eisenhower said:

You are about to embark upon the great crusade toward which we have strived for many months. The eyes of the world are upon you. The hopes and prayers of liberty-loving peoples everywhere are with you. You will bring about the destruction of the German war machine, the elimination of Nazi tyranny over the oppressed peoples of Europe and security for ourselves in a free world. Your task will not be an easy one. Your enemy is well-trained, well equipped and battle hardened. He will fight savagely but this is the year 1944. Much has happened since the Nazi triumphs of 1940-41. The United Nations have inflicted upon the Germans great defeat in open battle man to man. Our air offensive has seriously reduced their strength in the air and their capacity to wage war on the ground. Our home fronts have given us an overwhelming superiority in weapons and munitions of war and placed at our disposal great resolve of trained fighting men. The tide has turned. The Freemen of the world are marching together to Victory. I have full confidence in your courage, devotion to duty and skill in battle. We will accept nothing less than full victory. Good luck and let us all ask the Blessing of Almighty God upon this great and noble undertaking.

Adm. Royal E. Ingersoll, Commander in Chief of U.S. Atlantic Fleet, revealed that U.S. battleships, cruisers and destroyers from his command, had arrived in British waters in ample time to participate in covering our operations and in shore bombardment.

President Roosevelt said the whole country was tremendously thrilled but he hoped they would not gain too much over-confidence as this would destroy the war effort. He added the war was not over by any means nor was this operation over.

The Russian Ambassador made the following remarks: "This is very good and encouraging news. The catastrophe of Fascist Germany is drawing nearer. What Hitler and his criminal colleagues have dreaded most has happened. Germany is forced to carry on the war on two fronts. The Soviet people wish all success to our Allies in this most important military undertaking which is speeding up our common victory over the mortal enemy of mankind."

Quinton Reynolds in a statement made on his broadcast said that the war (which he called the invasion of Normandy) started on the sixth hour of the sixth day of the sixth month in contrast to the ending of World War I, which ended on the 11th hour of the eleventh day of the eleventh month of the year.

Many of us have relatives and friends in the invasion of France. Let us stand uncovered before Almighty God, silently asking for a speedy and righteous victory.

And now back to our little world. At 0114 last night a friendly surface craft was sighted. At 0700 the destroyer *Halsey Powell* reported an underwater contact on their port bow at a distance of 800 yards. We executed two emergency turns to starboard. A later report stated that it was not a submarine. This was most fortunate for if the contact had proven to be enemy it would have been within our convoy. The rumor of depth charges today has not been verified.

With all the big news from Europe today most of us have forgotten that we passed this morning right under the noses of the Japanese. At the closest point we were about 100 miles from Maloelap. Now we are through the Ratak Chain and will reach within possible sight of Kwajalein tomorrow morning. Friday about 0800 we are due to arrive at Eniwetok.

Now for a lighter vein. The judges have announced the winners of the poetry contest. The winner was Pfc. Charles P. Pase, Battery D, 2nd Bn., and honorable mention was awarded to Cpl. Jack Robinson. There were not a sufficient number of short stories submitted to judge.

Amen! until tomorrow.

Westward   June 8, 1944

Good evening shipmates.

You will remember a few nights ago I told you that we might have a chance to become acquainted with some of our observers. Tonight we are unusually fortunate to have aboard, Colonel Kemp of the British Army. Colonel Kemp is an expert in amphibious warfare and has been in on the planning of the invasion of Europe. He has consented to act as commentator regarding recent developments in that theatre. Colonel Kemp: (here follows the Colonel's address):

With the information received that Allied Forces have landed in Northern France on the morning of June 6th the following further comments may be of interest:

You may have noticed before June 6 that our news sheets emphasized the fact that Allied Air Forces had been making very heavy raids on the coastal strip near Calais and Boulogne, where the English Channel is narrowest (approximately twenty miles). Undoubtedly these raids in the north were part of a deception plan because we know now that the main assault was in fact not carried out here but further to the south of Normandy, where the channel is eighty to ninety miles wide.

This would be a less obvious place for a landing since the Nazis might reasonably be expected to be less prepared to meet invasion, than further north. This could mean that Allied Forces would meet with a less elaborate system of beach defenses and a less strongly held coast line and still be within the range of cover provided by fighter aircraft based in England.

We can picture perhaps some five assaulting divisions, possibly two USA, two British and one Canadian preceded by minesweepers and escorts. The Infantry will have been carried across the channel in small APA's, being transferred to LCV(P)'s about nine miles away from the enemy-held coast. Other assault troops will have made the crossing all the way in very large numbers of LCT's whilst reserves will have been in LCI's and LST's.

During the night before the assault there will have been an intense aerial bombardment, naval bombardment and landing Airborne troops. The landings themselves were apparently effected in daylight under an immense air umbrella, supported by further air bombing and by very intense naval bombardment, and by fire from all kinds of small gun craft mounting different types of weapons up to 4.7 inches, by rocket craft, and to insure that all available fire power was made use of, even by land artillery firing from LCT's as they came in. Although casualties appear to have been slight it is certain that these groups will have had to contend with many artificial obstacles put up by the Nazis; concrete walls up to ten feet thick and ten feet high — concrete pill boxes — steel scaffolding — wire — mines and many others. To get through these the assaulting infantry will probably have been preceded by tanks, some carrying assault engineers equipped with special demolition charges, others being tanks to give covering fire while the engineers did their work.

So much for the assault, but in an operation like this, assault is only a means to an end. That is not the only phase that counts. To defeat the German armies on the continent a large Army with its Air Force will have to be landed and assembled ashore with gigantic quantities of ammunition, gasoline, food and other commodities. During the weeks that are ahead we can picture a continuous shuttle service, going on day and night, across the English Channel, of men and material. Undoubtedly the object will be to expand the initial bridgehead so as to capture and bring into use as early as possible the important port of Cherbourg and maybe others. But in the English Channel even in the summer continued good weather for the landing of reserves over the beaches cannot be relied upon so that a port is vital, and we should be unwise to expect that such rapid advances as we have already seen will go on all the time. Determined German counter-attacks are certain, but provided the Allies can withstand these and make good their bridgehead during the first few weeks, the advance to Germany itself can be confidently looked forward to.

There is very little news from the ship tonight. At 0730 two friendly surface craft were sighted. This afternoon we all enjoyed the good fights and entertainment on top of No. 4 hatch and we thank the participants and committee for their good work. Tomorrow at about 0800 we are due to arrive at Eniwetok. Here we will be sorry to see the officers and men leave us for LST's. We know you go by order and not by preference. We will not see you until D-day so we sincerely wish you God-speed. It is in your honor that I read the prize-winning poem tonight. "Westward" by Pfc. Charles P. Pase:

To the west the sun was setting,
Sinking, o'er the throne of Mars.
So we stood in dimming twilight —
Turned our faces to the stars.

Thus we prayed to God Almighty,
That he give us strength and sustance;
For to west our faith might falter,
Where the dying sun lay down.

What cared we for wealth or glory?
What cared we for despot's power?
Then would God above forsake us;
Leave us perish and go down.

For our cause was something higher.
Even greater than the nation
Who had sent her sons to battle
Where the evening sun went down.

Then we felt a greater power
Which came down to us from Heaven.
Then we knew we would not falter —
God decreed our cause was just!

So to westward we are sailing,
Grave of heart, withal rejoicing;
Soon we make our final landing;
Let, in peace, the sun go down.

Then let all men band together;
Tempered bands through fear and pain —
Let all men be sure of justice;
God forbid we die in vain!

Amen! until tomorrow.

Eniwetok: Preview To Saipan   June 9, 1944

Good evening shipmates.

The early birds this morning were greeted by a worm-eaten battle cite that is not exactly forgotten. As we entered the lagoon of the Brown atolls by the east channel we passed on the port side, Parry Island where the main enemy fortifications were located just four months ago. Death still seemed to hang in the air as we saw at close range what the giant lawn mower of a naval and aerial bombardment can do. Hardly a single palm appeared alive amid the newer quonset huts, tents, and coral fortifications of the occupying troops. PBY's and PBM's were anchored off the seaplane runway, probably built by our CB's.

Joined by a reef with Parry Island but just out of our range of vision was the larger island of Eniwetok itself, containing the large Army Liberators that we saw winging overhead. As if in contrast to these man-made scenes of destruction was the little island of Japtan on the starboard side of the entrance. Here were the palms, breadfruit trees and foliage to remind us that these islands were the homes of some 120 brown, naked Kanakas, innocent victims of the fruits of war. Some of us wondered where they were now. What payment in sorrow, broken homes, and death had come to bewilder their simple life? Total war, learned by the English, and especially the citizens of London in those dreadful days of 1940-41, and now by our enemies in Berlin and twice-over by our allies in war-ridden France. This is no war of armies and navies alone but of whole peoples, women and children alike, old men and the physically unfit. The citizens of Eniwetok might have been citizens of Grovers Corners, USA, but for the grace of God, accidents of geography, and military strategy.

This brings me to a subject new to American forces. You will remember that in Africa, Sicily and Italy we found the citizens welcoming us with open arms. In only rare instances was there opposition from civilians. We also know that hereto-fore in the Pacific we have generally re-conquered Allied territory and fortunately found the natives cooperative in driving out the common enemy.

In the operation against the Marianas we are striking for the first time against the Japanese homeland where we expect to encounter, not only about 20,000 enemy troops and probably a few thousand more home-guard but perhaps 25,000 Japanese and Korean men, women and children who have worked, farmed and built their homes there. Saipan, Tinian and Rota will be the chief problems. In Guam our forces can expect cooperation from the Chamorros who are American nationals and speak English. They will be warned by leaflets to stay away from installations and military objectives. However, in Saipan we do not know just what to expect from the civilian population.

The simple minded will, of course, say anyone with a Japanese face should be shot. This would include innocent woman and children. Another type of simple mind, no less dangerous because of strong humanitarian sympathies, will seek to traffic with the civilians just as if they were Japanese-Americans in Honolulu. Intelligence officers have informed us that we are likely to find old and young alike indoctrinated with the idea that capture by the Americans means hideous torture. It is also possible that some unscrupulous commander, anxious to win an honored seat in Hades, will use innocent civilians as a screen for military purposes. In any case therefore, we must assume neither innocence nor guilt on the part of a civilian, but let their own actions determine our action against them.

We must also remember, that whereas the Germans and Japanese have earned most of their reputations for atrocities in combat areas inhabited by large numbers of civilians, we, so far in this war have not gained any reputation, good or bad, for the treatment of civilians. Our actions on Saipan will give us and, through us, all Americans, a reputation for generations to come. We will not lower ourselves to their level. We will preserve, insofar as military measures allow, a practice of decency and common sense.

Two air alerts make it hardly necessary for me to remind you that we are within bombing distance of strong enemy air bases. Though our planes are constantly pounding and paralyzing the Carolines, we cannot afford to relax our vigilance for a moment. We are about 350 miles from Ponape and about 700 miles from Truk.

The LST's pulled out this afternoon to resume their snail's pace toward the target. They have a headstart in order that we may all reach the target area at the same time on D day.

Amen! until tomorrow.

Civilian Sidelights   June 10, 1944

Good evening shipmates.

> *What care we where we may be,*
> *Oran, Algeria, Eniwetok or Hawaii;*
> *If only we get our mail.*

What care we for war's alarms
Or Willy who may bring us harm;
If only we get our mail.

As you can readily tell, I am no poet. But I imagine you get the idea. At one time it seemed as though the Fleet Post Office had never heard of the *Frederick Funston*. Now they can't wait to give us their personal attention. Whether it was Davisville, Norfolk, Balboa or Pearl Harbor we enjoyed the results of the battle cry, "The mail must go through!" Oh, if the folks back home only knew what they were receiving for six cents. Eniwetok, the end of the world, in one week from the east coast. Think of it! Among the few things we will remember about this war with any real pleasure, is "mail call." Scuttlebutt has it that there is a wager going around the ship with the odds about 50-50 to the effect that on D-1 there will be mail for the Freddy on the dock at Saipan.

After last night's talk I was correctly reminded that there is a distinction between a Korean and a Chamorro civilian and the Japanese civilians on Saipan. So I hasten to add a post-script on this important problem. My authority on the Korean situation is Mr. San Kap Kho, of Honolulu, who is aboard our ship on this campaign for the express purpose of dealing with this situation. Mr. Kho was born in Korea and speaks English, Korean and Japanese. Kho informs me that since the Russo-Japanese War of 1904-05, when Japan occupied and then gradually annexed Korea, there has been no love lost between the Koreans and the Japanese. Long before Japan went to work on China she was exploiting Korea and suppressing all movements or signs of independence. The Koreans are a distinct nationality with a language and culture of their own that goes back to the twelfth century B.C. Like the Chinese, Filipinos and others, they too desire to free themselves from Japanese domination. Leaflets have been printed especially for the Korean laborers on Saipan. Mr. Kho will broadcast to them over powerful loud speakers. He expects them to be of great value to us in supplying intelligence with information and in turning against their overlords.

The Chamorros are also a distinct, though minor group. They have houses of balconied, tropical-Spanish style. As one of the most interesting races of the Pacific, it was their ancestors on the Philippines who gave Magellan such a warm reception that he was killed. Then they came over to the Marianas and interbred with the emigrees from Malay. Their color is light, their language is half Spanish, their women wear the long skirts and balloon sleeves of the Philippines, and their men play guitars. As contrasted with the Japanese they are very gay and musical. Their homes have none of the exclusiveness of the Japanese home. Strangers just walk in whenever they hear music from a Chamorro home. They love to dance but there are no reports as to whether boogy-woogy has been introduced. Whereas the Japanese are usually Buddhists or Shintoists, the Chamorros are Catholics.

I think I will close this subject by giving you a general picture of the chief city, Garapan. The streets of the port are choked with charcoal-burning automobiles and primitive ox-carts. The 6,000 buildings include thatched huts of the Kanakas, substantial stone houses left over from the German regime — looking as if they had been built for a land of storm and snow — and modern Japanese stores. An old Spanish mission contrasts sharply with nearby radio towers, dried-bonita factories, and a half-mile of geisha houses.

I don't need to tell you what geisha houses are, but you might wonder what dried-bonita is. It is sun-baked fish that becomes hard as wood. It is considered a great delicacy to the housewife who shaves off a few thin shavings then adds to the family soup.

A good suggestion has been made. If you have questions that can be answered, write them out and leave them in the chaplain's office. The important ones will be answered if possible during the next few broadcasts.

Amen! until tomorrow.

Good evening shipmates.

This is D-3. By this time you have been anxious for more details on the operation against the Marianas. You know already that there are two task forces, the northern force of which we are a part, and the southern force. The northern force will take and occupy Saipan and Tinian. The southern force will take and occupy Guam. In our force the 2nd and 4th Marine Divisions are the assault troops and the 27th Army Division is the reserve. However, the assault on Guam by the 3rd Marine Division and 1st Prov. Brig. will not commence until it has been ascertained that they are not needed against Saipan. As you can see, this means that we must take Saipan at all costs. There are no plans for withdrawal. Guam follows next in importance and then Tinian and Rota.

The first blows against Saipan and Tinian were launched today, supposedly by land-based bombers from Eniwetok, composed of the 7th AAF. It is not known exactly what targets will be sought out today but we can assume a general all-around pasting. Also propaganda leaflets will be dropped today for the purpose of lowering the resistance of the civilians and getting them out of the way as well as to lower the resistance of the troops and eventually increase the number of prisoners on D-day and following.

On D-2 the bombardment will begin in real earnest by both aerial and naval units. Land-based bombers and 2,000 planes carried by fifty-three carriers will carry the aerial offensive. Specific objectives will be the coastal defenses, the burning of the sugar cane fields (where the whole army could hide), the destruction of buildings on the largest airfield (ASLITO) on the southern coast, and the destruction of communication and transportation facilities on the west coast.

The exact amount of aerial opposition that will be encountered is not known. Early estimates of the total enemy plane strength in the Marianas and Carolines was about 400. There are three airfields on Saipan. ASLITO is in the south and is capable of handling bombers. There is a new runway in the north and one on the west coast near the preferred assault beach. At least one field for bombers exists on Tinian, a few miles away. However, we are also within bombing range of other Japanese bases.

On D-2 and D-1, twelve of the total of eighteen battleships will also begin a bombardment with long range penetrating fire and short range direct fire on Saipan and Tinian. The targets are enemy guns and emplacements, to destroy aircraft and disable airfields, destroy enemy reserves and prevent their movement, lay down a harassing fire, to burn sugar cane fields, destroy enemy fuel dumps, destroy the town of Charan-Kanoa, and provide covering fire for underwater demolition teams.

It is known from recent reconnaissance photographs that the enemy has added considerably to their defenses and forces in the past two months. Large transports have been sighted in the harbor of Garapan and additional seaplanes, four-engine bombers and coastal guns are evident.

I have been asked to state the difference between a convoy and a task force. A convoy is any ship or group of ships under a protecting escort. We are therefore a convoy. A task force is a convoy or several convoys accompanied by warships who set out upon a particular task. We are a part of task force 52.

At 1704 tonight Willy showed up twenty-five miles ahead. Details later.

Last night another bit of drama was enacted in our convoy. The destroyer *Cony* reported an officer seriously ill with abdominal pains. He was ordered transferred to the transport *Feland*. The two ships then left the convoy under escort and made the transfer in a small boat. The transfer was completed by 1924.

Throughout the ship there are first aid boxes marked by a large Red Cross. You all know where they are and what they are for. Heretofore they have been kept locked. Now they are unlocked so that you and I can receive emergency treatment immediately. If something is missing from that box, any one of us might suffer unnecessarily. While we are on the subject it wouldn't be a bad idea if we all broke out our Bluejacket's Manuel tonight and refreshed our minds with chapter 28. Nobody can know too much on the subject of First Aid or be too careful with their medical equipment.

Troops are reported to be clogging passageways when general quarters is sounded. No matter where you are, step out of the way, clear a passage for the ship's company. When they have passed you can then lay below.

Our course is west-north-west. At 1800 tonight we were 700 miles from Saipan.

Amen! until tomorrow.

Preferred Plan   June 13, 1944

Good evening shipmates.

This is D-2. Throughout the day, tonight and tomorrow, right up to H hour the aerial and naval bombardment will continue their devastation of enemy installations. There will be no mistake as in the case of Salerno nor any "pulling of punches" as in the case of Tarawa. What the enemy dropped on Pearl Harbor and Wake will be exceeded many times over before the hour arrives for the Marines to land on Saipan.

Tomorrow one outfit will go into the reefs under a covering fire for the purpose of locating mines and under water defenses. These underwater demolition teams might be called "John the Baptists" because not only do they work underwater but they will "prepare the way." If they are successful there will be fewer "water buffalos" and landing boats that fail to reach the beach. They will be the first units to touch Saipan.

In the preferred plan for landings at Charan-Kanoa there are five beaches: red, 1, 2, and 3, and green 1, and 2. The 2nd Division will land on these beaches and the 4th Division on the blue and yellow beaches to the right. First landings will be made on green 1 and 2 beaches at H-hour with two LVT's abreast. These will be followed by landing on beaches red 2 and 3.

At the same time as the real operation is going on, there will be a diversionary operation above Garapan at Tanapag Harbor. After the main operation is underway these men from the 2nd Marines (regiment) will land on the preferred beaches.

In general, the immediate objectives are for the 2nd Division to seize Mt. Topotchau and the 4th Division to seize ASLITO airfield. Once the beaches are secured the artillery and support units will follow. However this is the first operation in which the divisional artillery will go ashore with the troops.

Counter-attacks can be expected by land, sea and air. For example the enemy is prepared to launch a counter-attack by small boats against any beach which we may have taken. They will do everything in their power to drive us back into the sea. All of their possible channels for counter-attack have been taken into consideration and covered by our forces.

As you already know, LVT's or "water buffalos" are being used to overcome the difficult obstacle in the reef. There is a passage about eighteen feet wide in the reef that can be used for LCM's and LCV(P)'s when it is cleared of mines and the guns covering it have been taken care of.

Here is one item of first-rate importance for all men who will go on the beach. It is necessary to have a system of passwords in order to prevent mistaken identity and infiltration tactics. For the first five days the password is any month of the year. Thus Marine Joe challenges sailor John, "Halt, who is there?" John will answer April and Joe will in return say June. It is well to vary the month and, if necessary, challenge again using a different month. In the second five days you will use any large cities. In the third five days any large state will save you from getting an unnecessary slug.

We were all interested enough in the fueling operation today to stand for some hours watching the transport destroyer *Noa* and the destroyer *Pritchett* heave to. The *Noa* created the greater interest because of the *Breecher's* buoy shuttling across from our after boat deck loaded with ice cream, bread, books, other necessities and luxuries. It seems the baking ovens of the *Noa* broke down. Of no less interest was the impressing array of battle flags on her bridge. They stood for two German subs sunk, five probables, two bombardments of Japanese defenses and six raids or campaigns. As best we could make out, the latter included Cape Gloucester, Saidor, Green Island, Aitape, Emireau and Seleo.

Japanese medium bomber "Sally" chased away at 1730 eighty miles away.

All library books borrowed by troops are due at 1200 tomorrow. The last divine services to be held for awhile will be on the starboard promenade deck tomorrow afternoon. At 1500 Protestant Services and Holy Communion and at 1600 Catholic Mass and Holy Communion.

Amen! until tomorrow.

D-1   **June 14, 1944**

TO THE OFFICERS
AND MEN OF THE SECOND MARINE DIVISION:

The missions assigned to the Marine Corps, throughout its history, have been those which have been determined must be accomplished expeditiously and efficiently. The task now before us is another "must". We are proud to help do the job. Just as in previous operations we breached the wall of the Japanese outer ring of defenses, we shall now crash through the inner defense line by the destruction of the enemy forces on Saipan.

You have trained hard and well. You are prepared to demonstrate the best teamwork this Division has ever known. You will be fighting side-by-side with another battle-tried

Marine Division; units of the United States Army are fighting with us; and, the finest and greatest naval force in history supports us.

I join every officer, soldier, sailor and marine in their complete faith and confidence in your swift and complete success in the capture of our objective.

To each of you, GOOD LUCK!

T. E. WATSON,
Major General, U.S. Marine Corps,
Commanding.

These words make us aware that after five weeks aboard our ship we are about to part company with the 2nd Marine Division. You are the first Marines to be aboard the *Funston* and you have acquited yourselves well in the eyes of the officers and crew. If you have successfully survived the grease-cable "booby traps" and the labyrinth of endless ladders and passageways, you ought to be in good shape for Saipan. We haven't meant to be hard on you, though at times it may have seemed we forgot you were guests. You did growl a little when you only got one free scoop of ice cream instead of two though we imagine you were sorry when you saw the ship's crew give their share to the *Noa* yesterday. When all is said and done we give you a lot of credit for landing on that beach while we remain relatively safe on our ship. We would never admit it, of course, but we do admire you for the part you will play in the final victory and we will be only too glad to take you home again whenever you finish your job.

At this moment we are less than seventy-five miles, by the way the crow flies, from our target. However, you have probably guessed that we are making a wide circle to the north and will come in on the west side of the island. By 0600 we will be in the transport area about ten miles off the beach. H-hour is at 0830 tomorrow.

This afternoon friendly planes dropped floating parcels containing last minute information. They were picked up by minesweepers and delivered to the *Cambria* and *Monrovia*.

We ought to see tomorrow morning some of the eighteen battleships, fifty-three carriers, thirty-three cruisers and many, many destroyers which have, and will continue, to shell the beach. Among the battlewagons you may recognize the *California, Pennsylvania, Tennessee, Maryland, Colorado, Idaho* and *New Mexico*. Those will carry on the greater part of the bombardment together with the cruisers *Indianapolis, Birmingham, Louisville, Montpelier, Cleveland, Honolulu, Minneapolis, San Francisco, Wichita* and *New Orleans*. Of these ships there are certain ones assigned to bombard each beach. For our beaches the battleship *California*, cruiser *Birmingham*, and destroyers *Coghlan, Monssen* and *Halsey Powell* are assigned.

I hope you did not forget the information I gave you on passwords last night. For the first five days if you are challenged, "Halt, who is there?" you will say _____ , that's right, the name of a month. The second five days, a large city and the third five days, a state. Now here is some more information that we hope you will never have to use. In the event you are taken prisoner, you MUST give your name, rank and identity number. Nothing else of any kind should be divulged.

World news is scarce tonight. The reason is that the battleship *Pennsylvania* is using the same frequency that we receive news on, for her bombardment of Saipan. That is good news in itself. A few moments ago the radio shack heard her talking to her fire-control plane. "Give me the bearings," she said, "on the ammunition dump with the red cross on it." (Later it was verified that this hospital, though not an ammunition dump itself, was located in the center of gun emplacements and four dumps. Even then it was avoided by dive bombers because of the Red Cross on its roof).

It is customary before entering an engagement to offer Prayer:

> *Eternal Father, strong to save, grant, we pray Thee, for*
> *our country, and for the benefit of the world in general,*
> *a complete and righteous victory; may no misconduct in*

*anyone tarnish it; and may humanity after victory
dominate our every action.*

*For ourselves individually, we commit our lives to
Him who made us; to the trust our loved-ones have placed
in us; and to the just cause which we are privileged to
defend.*

*For these things we pray through our Lord, who is
our strength.*

Amen! until tomorrow.

The Cost Of War   June 18, 1944

Good evening shipmates.

Much water has passed under the bridge since I last brought
you any full announcements. Even today, which is D plus 3,
there is not very much to pass along. The last casualties that
came aboard yesterday brought news which pretty well established the fact that our troops have reached the top of the ridge,
visible to the south of Mt. Topatchau. Casualties yesterday
were much lighter as compared to D-day and D plus 1.

You are probably wondering by what strange reason we
deserve this Sunday rest. It seems that Friday, units of our
fleet reported enemy warships headed toward Saipan. They
went out to intercept them. We have not heard as yet the
results. Nevertheless it was decided as a safety precaution to
remove the transports from the danger zone. We did not move
too soon. There was an enemy air raid last night almost as
soon as our wake settled behind us. Throughout evening
general quarters the heavy and colorful ack-ack rose from our
fleet in the harbor. It was reported that a ship in the convoy
forming on our stern was hit. We will return as soon as the
danger has passed for we still have over half our cargo to
unload.

Nevertheless this day has been a God-send to weary men and our precious cargo of wounded. The three "busy-Bees", Drs. Barrett, Brooks and Bryer, plus the able assistance of Marine doctors, Dr. Cappetto, ship and Marine corpsman, are doing a tireless and magnificent job in caring for our over 200 wounded Marines. It is safe to say that nearly all are out of danger and quite comfortable. Most of them are able to get around on their own power already and are assisting the corpsmen with the care of their shipmates.

The best way we can all help these veterans convalesce is to keep quiet in the vicinity of the sickbays. The wounded are in officer's country on A deck, on B deck aft, and B deck forward on port side as well as in sickbay and hold 2-C. Unless you are on specific and necessary business, use these areas as little as possible for passageways. If you have gifts of magazines or cigarettes for them, leave them in the library or chaplain's office.

Last night it was reliably reported that a body, identified by one officer as a Japanese, passed on our starboard side. The night before, as we got underway, some of you may have noticed the Japanese assault boat bobbing around empty on the starboard side. Very early Friday morning, early risers were able to view a short but sweet naval engagement on the horizon to the northwest of Saipan. As best we can learn, several enemy cargo ships tried to get in and supply the island under cover of darkness. By daybreak they were all burning and sinking.

We were all curious about the five-year-old Japanese child who was brought aboard Friday with slight wounds on his left arm. Despite the interpreters and the excellent care he received, the boy was too frightened to speak. The same afternoon he was returned to the beach under the care of Mr. Kho and Lt. Sheek with the intention of placing him in the care of a civilian woman. They got no further than the beach for a barrage was laid down at that time and the boy became lost in the confusion and rush for cover.

All of us are saddened at the news of the death of our shipmate Don Edwin Woods, Slc, of the navy beach party. Woods worked in the 2nd Division and then in the laundry and was well liked by all who knew him. He is the first *Funston* man to give his life for his country and freedom.

For those of you who have lost all track of time this is Father's Day, Sunday, 18th of June.

Amen! until tomorrow.

We Discover Saipan   June 22, 1944

Good evening shipmates.

Since very few of us were able to take that prospective liberty in Saipan and about the same number actually got around over there, yours truly tried to act as your eyes this morning and bring you an eye-witness account of conditions in the conquered area, exactly one week after D-day.

A fact which all the boat crews will verify is the noticeable number of amtracs, tanks and alligators caught on the reef as any of the beaches are approached. They just sit there mutely looking as if they were in any American barnyard and about as useful.

We went ashore at the pier of the sugar-cane mill at Charan-Kanoa. This is yellow beach. To the right on yellow beach they have already constructed a dock of pontoons and are unloading on it. To the right of the pontoon dock I counted ten wrecked assault boats, grim reminders of those counter-attacks which took place while we were at sea.

The pier itself was re-captured by the enemy on D plus 1 and re-captured again by the Marines immediately afterward. It is wrecked but usable after the CB's worked it over. The sugar mill looks like the center of Berlin. Just a mess of twisted steel and concrete blocks. It still gives out that sweet but sickening odor that was blown our way last evening. And lest we think this wiley enemy doesn't make use of their opportunities, that innocent looking smokestack that is still standing was used as a fire-control tower until we discovered there was more in it than soot. Despite the many holes in it and our bombardment of the factory those men sat up there several days directing fire on the beaches. Let's move along.

We hitched a ride in a jeep and headed south along the shore through Charan-Kanoa. Hardly a single building was still intact and no civilians were visible anywhere. We were told that children were running around, however. Most of the houses were very flimsy, consisting of a frame and woven bamboo walls, chocked with red clay. The better homes, where the colonists evidently lived, were quite stably built of concrete and plastered walls. The oriental homes are all so different from our occidental homes. The floor is raised high and the windows low. There are mats on the floor where the people slept and stubby little tables where they took their meals while sitting cross-legged on the floor. Most of the homes had electricity, drew their water from cisterns in the rear and used privies for plumbing. They were not WPA style privies either. Any useable buildings now house headquarters offices. Troops had made over some others and were sleeping in them. It looked funny to see them cooking on the little cement stoves and trying to figure ways to use the dishes and utensils left behind. The tea they found was reported very good and I did see many empty saki bottles.

We were surprised to see so many prisoners. There was one stockade for soldiers down near yellow beach and another reported for civilians near the airstrip. We passed a column of twenty that looked like they might be home guard, marching up the road under two tough Marines. At another place we saw two being brought in and a well-cared-for wounded Japanese went by in an ambulance jeep. At no time were any unburied bodies visible but a few animals were still laying around competing with the sugar mill for control of the air waves.

All kinds of traffic moved down the shore road but we turned off after about a mile and headed inland for the Aslito airfield. Many of the men were relaxing from the fighting in this area and were helping each other take well-needed baths. The dust is heavy, as you may have noticed from the artillery bursts.

All around us there was artillery fire from our own batteries pounding their way up to the front line, about one-half mile up the side of Mt. Topatchau. Now the barrage you heard this morning was a full-scale blast of what has been going on all day and will continue to give the Japanese a bit of their own medicine. The situation is reversed for there was no return of artillery fire in this sector.

All along the way to the airfield the men were putting the trimmings on their Waldorf-Astoria suites. There was plenty of lumber and cane around and some of them had harnessed big black oxen, of the water-buffalo variety, and had them pulling little two-wheel carts for them. The oxen didn't know what was going on because few of the GIs could speak Japanese, but the Iowa farm boys looked like they had the situation well in hand.

Aslito airfield is a real prize and no fooling. You can realize that from the number of Thunderbolts above us tonight. We stood there as our army land-based planes pulled off, thankful for our control of the skys. They should be able to use it for bombers very shortly though right now fighters, cubs and dive-bombers had it to themselves. Most surprising were the large number of enemy planes captured on the ground. The Japanese got out of there so fast they even left their toothbrushes behind for the souvenir hunters. Though our bombardment was everywhere in evidence there were at least twenty Zeroes that can soon be put into use if necessary. They didn't look very formidable sitting there on the runway but as one pilot said, "They look much bigger in the air." The prize in the airdrome, besides the Zekes, was a larger job fitted with radar. This seemed important enough to the Japanese for them to return on the second night and try to destroy it. Most of the buildings on the airfield, including the hangers are in useable condition. Their frames still stand intact and with new roofs and sides they will house planes, be used for barracks and offices. Regretably, one of the buildings nearby that was hit in the bombardment, was a hospital with a large Red Cross on the roof. Located as it was, among barracks and airfield buildings, it could hardly have escaped the naval fire. Shrapnel was laying around everywhere, some pieces as large as your arm, attesting to the terrific fire that had been directed toward this strategic objective.

The other airstrip, near the beach that our navy beach party became so well acquainted with, is in use also. I will tell you more of what went on there when I hear and confirm all the stories of our shipmates who are now back aboard. One believe-it-or-not sight was a Grumman torpedo bomber turned upside down and resting on an amtrac to the side of the field. It was one of those freaks of war, like those four fellows in sickbay with bullet holes through their helmets, that can keep us smiling when we think about them.

As we watch the sun setting on the "land of the sinking sun" tonight you are asking where we are headed and how long it will take to get there. To the best of our knowledge we are headed for Pearl Harbor and we will take about twelve days getting there.

Amen! until tomorrow.

Scuttlebutt Or News   June 23, 1944

Good evening shipmates.

The big news tonight comes from the battle of the task forces. It did not last long for our air arm of carrier planes which began the attack, sank a Japanese carrier, three tankers and possibly a destroyer and damaged nine or ten other ships in a surprise attack between the Philippines and the Marianas. The engagement was broken off by the Japanese fleet which fled during the night toward the channel between Formosa and Luzon.

47

The carrier task force under the immediate command of Vice Admiral Marc V. Mitscher had no losses and only forty-nine planes, many of which were forced to land in the water at nightfall, were lost. Many pilots may have been rescued. In the Japanese futile attempt on Adm. Mitscher's force Sunday (Monday our time) 352 enemy planes were shot down. Two U.S. carriers and one battleship suffered superficial damage. Twenty-one of our aircraft were lost in that combat.

Tonight I want to mention some important details on the operation on Saipan, which have been gathered from one source or another of reliable information, and which were omitted last night. As all of us are becoming increasingly aware, the weird tales and fantastic scuttlebutts are already having the platform. How false rumors begin is a great mystery, but like the poor, they are always among us. The beach party heard a succession of such reports, such as Tinian and Guam having been captured and Russia declaring war on Japan, etc. So many of the stories about Saipan are pure fantasy. Others have some basis in fact and grow in detail as they are told. I say this only as introduction because no one is invulnerable from a good, juicy piece of scuttlebutt.

The last casualties aboard reported the chief difficulty encountered in the hills was ferreting the enemy out of caves, some as deep as 100 yards. If anyone is under any illusions as to how short this war may be, let them consider how many caves there are to be cleaned out in the rest of the key bases of the enemy. Caves are playing an important part in the enemy's defense. The trick used in Guadalcanal of firing a few rounds of artillery and then running the gun back into a cave before planes could find it, was used to devastating effect upon us. The mysterious eight inch gun was mounted on tracks, run out, fired and then backed into a cave that was fitted with steel doors. By careful watch they finally got that one. Now they are using flame throwers, bazookas, grenades and other weapons to clean out these pockets of resistance on Mt. Topatchau.

On Tuesday night, which was the night before we returned to the harbor, snipers crept into the beach area and set off a huge ammunition dump with rifle fire. For about two hours from 2,100-2,300 shells and explosions were at their worst. The dump burned the rest of the night. Men who were near that explosion say that it threw them out of their foxholes and sent a sheet of flame as high as old Topatchau itself. It is reported that a pocket of snipers, supposedly the same that set off the dump, were still at large in the vicinity of Lake Susepe.

There were many camouflaged enemy trucks, buses, tankers and such, being used by our troops. All seemed modeled on the Ford variety except that they had right-hand instead of left-hand drive. Perhaps the most general means of transportation, however, were bicycles of English manufacture. Some were being used by tired Marines and others were noticed in LCV(P)'s, destined as souvenirs.

And speaking of souvenirs there is a good article on that subject in the Bureau of Naval Personnel Information Bulletin of January 1944. It will be well for you to read this new liberalized policy on the after recreation room bulletin board if you have any questions on the matter. Especially noticeable are the injunctions against having any kind of explosives in your gear. This is a protection for yourself and your shipmates as well. It was interesting to notice on the beach how the MPs were cracking down on souvenir hunters. Such men were immediately put on burying details. They did this not because they begrudged your having trophies of the war but because there was too much work to be done to have time for excursions.

I neglected to mention that at Aslito airfield, we captured not only a radar plane but a complete radar operation set that looked in usable condition.

You may not believe it but everywhere we went Marines and CBs from the *Funston* recognized us and waved to all like long lost brothers. Twice they stopped and said something like this, "We got off in too much of a hurry to thank whoever was responsible, but you tell them that that was the best

49

transport we were ever on and we've been on plenty." So that is a compliment to everyone of the ship's personnel and I have witnesses to prove it is a fact. The first men we talked to wanted to know what was the news from the outside world. They were hungry to know what was going on in France, Italy and even on the front just a few miles away. No wonder scuttlebutt gets started. If they can't get the news they manufacture it like Goebbels, the way they want it.

At the present time we have 180 wounded men aboard which we are taking to Pearl. All together we have cared for 267, over three times the number we ever had before. Though we have buried thirteen at sea you will rejoice with me to know that practically all wounded are now on the road to recovery.

If you are interested in a little play on letters tonight maybe you can find something significant in the letter "S". All the invasions the "Freddy" has participated in begin with "S": Sicily, Salerno and Saipan (to say nothing of Scotland). To add to the priority of the letter "S", the general in command of Marine landing operations is Lt. Gen. Holland M. Smith and the command of the 27th Army Division is another "S", Maj. Gen. Ralph C. Smith.

Our course is approximately east-southeast and our distance at 1800 from Pearl Harbor was 3,166. We are not going by way of Eniwetok, though we will be near. There will be a movie tonight in hold 2-C entitled "My Friend Flicka." All the comforts of home away from home!

This will be my last regular broadcast for awhile. If things come up from time to time I will be back on the air to tell you about them but until then I will say,

Amen, until later.

Change Of Command   June 26, 1944

Good evening shipmates.

At 1300 today Captain John E. Murphy, USN, turned over the command of our ship to Captain Charles C. Anderson,

USN. Captain Murphy has been our skipper since the ship was commissioned in April of 1943. It was necessary in less than three months to put the *Funston* in shape for a major invasion. That this was done successfully is of no small credit to a commanding officer. Thereafter we participated in a second major invasion and were in enemy waters for six months. After an overhaul in the yards we came into new enemy waters and have successfully carried out a third amphibious landing.

It is not our opinion alone but that of thousands of soldiers, CBs and Marines that we have a ship to be proud of. To think that initially practically all of us were landlubbers, with our sea duty confined to the Staten Island Ferry, is to comprehend what Captain Murphy's leadership has made of us in these fourteen months. We understand his new duty is still unknown. Whatever it is we wish our skipper Good Luck and Good Sailing!

Most of you are already acquainted with the sight of our new commanding officer, Captain Anderson, since he came aboard May 30th at Pearl Harbor. Captain Anderson is from Washington, D.C. He graduated from Annapolis Academy in 1919 and has served on nearly all types of ships since that time. Twelve of these years were spent in submarine duty. Our new skipper comes to us directly from the Bureau of Ships in Washington. He is married and has one son, a Sergeant in the 4th Marine Division. Sergeant Anderson was aboard the *Funston* at Eniwetok and is now at the front in Saipan. To Captain Anderson we extend a sincere welcome and our hearty cooperation in keeping the "Freddy" a happy ship.

Amen!

Man Overboard   **June 28, 1944**

Good evening shipmates.

When the U.S.S. *Talbot* heaved to along our starboard side this morning she didn't create any more than the usual interest at a fueling operation at sea. It was nice of her though to come along the starboard side so the convalescents out in the solarium could watch the operation. We also noted she carried a claim for two Japanese planes and participation in eight operations, had a smashed bow and one engine out. Then about 1200 the mouths of all *Funston* railbirds dropped open, and it wasn't for chow either. Somehow a *Talbot* sailor who was heaving in a hauling line was knocked overboard, yelling as he fell, "man overboard!" For a moment we didn't know whether he would be caught under the fuel hose or hauling lines but he bobbed up in his kapok lifejacket almost immediately. The first thing he seemed to do was guide himself away from the screw of the APD. We stopped our screw. Immediately the destroyer sent up her "man overboard" signal flag and ships to stern manuevered out of the way. It was the minesweeper *Champion* that picked him up a few minutes afterwards while all *Funston* mouths resumed their normal position.

Time marches backward! Tomorrow evening we re-cross the International Date Line. Now you can pull that day out of your pocket that you tore off around June 5th and put it back on the calender. You will not change the time on your watches. Many a man has said regretfully, "Ah, if I could only live that day over again!" Here is your big chance to see what you will do with it. At least one man, Bos'n. Mate first class Maxwell, gets two birthdays out of this.

Have you noticed our new campaign bar and star on the chest of our signal bridge? This is all rather elementary, but for those who never knew each of those colors it has a specific meaning. Starting from starboard to port we have the American theatre ribbon with its blue field representing the oceans flanking North America. On the sides are the black and white of Nazi Germany and the red and white of Japan. Each bar has red, white and blue colors in the center.

The second ribbon is the African-European theatre with green for the fields of Europe flanked by brown representing the sands of Africa. Black and white again for Nazi Germany and red, white and green for Italy. The latest addition to our collection is the Asiatic-Pacific theatre ribbon with yellow background for the far east and the red and white of Japan on the sides. Of course we all know what the stars stand for and realize their importance cannot be judged by their size. Though the latest star has come easier to the men of the *Funston* than the others, each distinguishes you nevertheless as a veteran who has fought against each of the Axis powers. You will have a right to wear each earned ribbon and star proudly in recognition of jobs well done.

Today we have received a few more pats on the back. From Adm. Somerville to Adm. Nimitz, "Congratulations to you and the Pacific fleet for a great victory." And from CincPac, "The prime minister of England and the First Sea Lord have sent to Adm. King messages of congratulations on the losses and damage inflicted on the Japanese." The storekeeper informs me if any more messages are received he will have to stock a larger size in hats.

Amen! until later.

Secure   **July 2, 1944**

Good evening shipmates.

This is the end of a long cruise and the last of these evening messages and news broadcasts until we shove off again. It was thirty-five long days ago that we shoved off from Pearl. We have covered 8,574 miles of ocean, most of it still inhabited by the enemy, by Willy, Bogie and the rest of the gang. We have participated in what may prove to be the most fatal of all blows yet struck at the Japanese. How fatal, we have yet to learn. We have, so to speak, been playing marbles for keeps in the enemy's back yard and we are returning with far more than we lost.

We must admit that we are extremely fortunate. With the one exception of Don Woods, we have suffered no casualties to either material or personnel. Of our three invasions this invasion of Saipan has been and still is one of the hardest fought battles of the war. Our precious load of casualties reminds us of that. Thankfully they too are coming through in fine shape although eighteen days aboard ship has been a strain on them. Out of the total 269 that we have cared for; twenty-three are Marine officers, 207 enlisted Marines, nineteen enlisted Navy, and twenty enlisted Army. Of all these we will have to put ashore only twelve in stretchers tomorrow. This is a tribute to our fine medical staff and corpsmen.

Thinking of all this mail that will be waiting for us tomorrow reminds me of a concrete building, half demolished, in Charan-Kanoa. On the outside was painted in bold lettering, "4th Marine Division, Saipan, M.I., Post Office". It didn't seem very busy and I wondered whether the sign might have been put up by the Morale Department. Anyway if we have to re-trace our wake within the next few weeks, we all hope it will be to fill that empty building in Charan-Kanoa with mail bags. And while I am on the subject, may I suggest that all hands stock up well with magazines before the next cruise. When you are through with them they mean a great deal to the wounded.

In case you have forgotten, day after tomorrow is the Fourth of July. If you have forgotten where you were or what you were doing the last Fourth, turn to chapter fourteen in John Mason Brown's, *To All Hands*.

I am sure all of us feel that we have already had enough of a celebration in the traditional manner. Instead of seeing how much noise we can make we will probably seek out a quiet spot with a copy of the Declaration of Independence or Thorne Smith or something.

If the Fourth seems like any other day this year maybe you can be eased with this thought. There are a lot of prisoners in the Philippines who have been there since Bataan fell two years ago. There are thousands of good, loyal Filipinos and millions of suffering Chinese and East Indians who won't be able to celebrate such a great day either. They are waiting for us. We hope they will not have to wait long. When their day of liberation comes then we will really celebrate the day of Independence, Freedom and Liberty. What a Glorious Fourth that will be and we will all feel a share in it.

In conclusion I would like to thank both Captain Murphy and Captain Anderson for the opportunity to give these broadcasts. They have spared nothing. No news has been withheld or censored, even information of great military importance. And you too have been very tolerant. You have smiled politely at some of my poor jokes. You have made polite suggestions for improvement that I hope have been incorporated. You have excused obvious difficulties in pronunciations of Japanese, Chinese, French, Burmese and Italian names and places. You have refrained from giving raspberries when Brooklyn lost a ball game. In all you are quite worthy of the salutation, "Shipmates."

There is no regular news tonight though a broadcast this afternoon spoke of enemy bombers striking against shore installations and transports on Saipan. No damage was mentioned. For further news consult your Honolulu *Star-Bulletin*.

We will moor at 0815 in Honolulu.

Amen! until the next cruise.

Guam

A compilation of broadcasts to ship's personnel and troops on board U.S.S. Frederick Funston (APA-89)

Anchors aweigh and we begin another long cruise westward today. Our able commander-in-chief sent us a message this afternoon which reads, "My confidence and best wishes to you and all under your command. Good hunting! Nimitz." What we are all asking now is, "where are the happy hunting grounds?" I wish we knew. What we do know is this, we are now headed for that paradise of the Pacific, that atoll of atolls, Eniwetok.

Men of the "Freddy" meet the men of the 77th Division. You remember rubbing elbows on King Street with soldiers wearing a statue of liberty on their left shoulder. Well, you are still rubbing elbows with them. The 77th was disbanded shortly after the last war and was re-formed about two years ago. Originally they were all from New York and New Jersey, hence their symbol. Now about seventy-five percent are from north of the Potomac and east of the Alleghenies. Their average age is twenty-eight.

We are carrying reserves, men of the 307th regiment, 2nd Battalion. There are special units also. All are under the immediate command of Lt. Col. C. F. Learner. These men have been trained in every possible type of warfare they might encounter in this area. This will be their first engagement but we are sure they will acquit themselves well. Since we only participate in invasions that begin with "S", we expect to land you at Singapore or Shanghai.

We come from everywhere. We are under the able command of Capt. C. C. Anderson. But we would prefer you would judge us by our ship. We are proud of her. She is clean, efficient and as happy as conditions allow. We have more room and more comforts than most ships of this type. We will try and treat you, not as cattle, or even as passengers, but as shipmates brought together by the fates of war.

Amen! until tomorrow.

It was a wonderful feeling to pick up the news and read of the end of the campaign on Saipan July 8. Except for the sting of snipers we can scratch that important base off the list and turn our attention to the remaining islands of the southern Mariana group. Adm. Harry E. Yarnell, USN, former commander of the Asiatic fleet, stated that with the occupation of Saipan, Japan's entire outer supply lines are threatened as well as much of her natural resources, needed to prosecute the war. Probably back home the fall of Caen, only 120 miles from Paris, will make the headlines but for us it is highly significant that Saipan was secured in only twenty-three days on a time schedule that called for twenty days.

Casualties will undoubtedly be high, as we know. In the first two weeks the casualties on Saipan were fifty percent those of the same period in Normandy. In proportion to the number involved they were higher than Normandy. As the correspondent in Yank said, Guadalcanal was tough, Tarawa was tougher but Saipan was the toughest going yet. Those 2nd and 4th Marines who constituted 7/8ths of the force and the 27th Army, who constituted 1/8th, deserve our highest respect.

You will remember that shortly after D-day on Saipan, the 3rd Marine Division and the 1st Prov. Marine Brigade were to attack Guam. That operation was of secondary importance to Saipan and they were held off until it was sure the primary objective was secured. Tinian and Rota have yet to be taken also. You want to know where we are going to come in on this second step. Where these two Marine outfits have been, we do not know. When they will strike, we do not know. But we do know that they will strike Guam soon and that the 77th Division will land on William plus 2 on another beach on the same island. So now you know where the "Hunting ground" is.

Best story of the cruise comes to us on sworn testimony of Lt. Pearson. It seems that sometime last night, a "bogie", which is an unidentified flying object, decided to land on our radar "bedspring". As the radar turned around, this "bogie" (be it seagull, albatross, or Japanese beetle) was having a high old time — like a kid on a merry-go-round. Well, either he had eaten a decaying sardine, had dysentery, got merry-go-round sick or just wanted to empty his bilges. Anyway men on watch said it looked as though the sky were filled with skimmed milk. In case you doubt the story, just ask the signalmen who had to swab it up. The area covered measured from No. 3 hatch to Nos. 1 and 2 davits. How did they get him off? Just gave the radar a quick reverse, of course.

Strange as it may seem a soldier stopped a sailor last night hurrying to general quarters. "What's general quarters, mac?" "Search me, buddy, I'm new here myself." Let's go back to the ABCs for a moment. We are in reach of enemy subs; "Willy" to you, and soon we will be in reach of enemy planes. The best time for attack is sunrise or sunset. So some of the ships in the convoy have general quarters at sunrise and others at sunset. At such times all battle stations are manned. Troops are to keep passageways clear until the crew has passed. Should the alarm sound at any other time than sunset, you can bet your life it won't be a drill.

Amen! until tomorrow.

How Deep Is The Ocean   July 11, 1944

This is our third day out. Still we have seen nothing but water and more water. It is difficult to grasp with our imagination the immensity of the gigantic space that is called the Pacific Ocean. If I were to say that the Pacific is 68,634,000 square miles, it wouldn't mean much. Even one square mile is difficult for many of us to visualize.

On that account it might be well to attempt some other measurement. For instance, it would take 258 states the size of Texas to equal the area of the Pacific Ocean, which is thirty-three times as great as our whole country.

In fact the Pacific is greater in area than all the land masses of the world combined. You could take Europe and Asia, Africa and Australia, North and South America, together with all the islands of all the seas and put them all in this big bathtub and there would still be room enough left over to put four times the area of the U.S.

Each group of islands is vast also. For example we thought we had left the Hawaiian islands last Sunday. Now today we find one of them just 105 miles off our port beam. That is where those planes you saw today came from, Johnston Island, just a little more than a line of surf and sand and coral large enough to land planes on. Nine hundred miles west and south of Honolulu, it remained for some time the furthest outpost of our Navy's airforce after Pearl Harbor.

Coming back to home, for after all what are millions of miles of water to us compared with the thousands of feet of ship which is our temporary home. After a little research we have dug up some information about our namesake that I think you might be interested in. Most of us have known as little about Frederick Funston as we do about this part of the world.

He was born in Ohio, son of an artillery officer in the Civil War. For two years he studied at the University of Kansas, later reported for the Kansas City *State Journal* and then became connected with the Department of Agriculture and was deputy comptroller of the Santa Fe Railroad. Later he made his home in Sante Fe.

Funston's military career began when he joined the fight for Cuban independence from Spain. He distinguished himself at La Machuca and was promoted to Lt. Col. Because of wounds and illness he tried to escape to the U.S. but he was captured by the Spanish and condemned to death. Finally, however, he was set free. When we entered the war Funston was sent to the Philippines where he performed the great feat of capturing the native insurrection leader Aquinaldo. During this campaign he rose to the rank of Brig. General. It may well be that history will find the name of Frederick Funston engaged in another Philippine campaign, this time assuring the liberation of a people, a liberation that began with the removal of Spanish mis-rule and native war lords, back in the days of the General.

On one occasion an army warrant officer added this to our knowledge of Gen. Funston. Just before World War I we had difficulties on the Mexican border with Pancho Villa and such. It was Gen. Funston who had charge of that expedition. In the meantime we came nearer to involvement in the European war. The General was slated to have command of the first American Expeditionary Force. Illness intervened however, and he died suddenly, to be succeeded by his second in command, General John J. Pershing.

As you can see we bear a great name; a name we share with the army and a name that has real significance in the Western Pacific.

Amen! until tomorrow.

Pearl Harbor Highway   July 12, 1944

Very little out of the ordinary has happened so far on this cruise. Unlike the last trip, the sea and sky seem to have given us little cause for alarm. Here is a summary of the convoy news to date. Our course lies on a "bee" line between Pearl Harbor and Eniwetok. We are *not* dipping away from Japanese-held Wake Island at all. We are *not* going through the Marshall's outer Radak chain as we did over a month ago.

Since every part of the ocean looks the same, sea going men are always giving names to certain areas or routes. You have heard of Torpedo Junction, Hell's Corner, Bomber's Row, etc. It has been suggested that this route be called "Pearl Harbor Highway." One reason for this moniker is that this is the route which men and supplies will use for some time to come in moving toward the finishing blows of the war in the

Pacific. Another reason is that we have already passed three different ships with their escorts, going in the other direction.

Tomorrow our route takes us into Oriental waters. About 0800 we are due to cross the International Date Line.

Amen! until tomorrow.

Guam, USA   July 13, 1944

It seems about time that we had some more information about our objective, Guam. And there is considerably more information available on Guam than there was on Saipan, which had been kept in a closet of secrecy by the Japanese for the past thirty years. But for forty-three years Guam was American, much to the enemy's displeasure, and during this time a good deal of data was collected about it. We have another more direct source of information also for one of our petty officers, Chief Pharmicist Mate Carney, had duty there before the war.

We described Saipan to you as a kangaroo sitting on its haunches. Guam is a little more difficult to picture. One man says it looks like a boomerang, another like a boot and third says it just looks like Guam. It is the southernmost and largest of the Marianas, being thirty miles from tip to tip and eight miles wide, twice the size of Saipan. With an hour glass figure it tapers to 3¼ miles just north of the center, then widens toward both ends, with the southern portion somewhat larger than the northern.

On the west coast of the southern half is Apra Harbor or Port Apra, formed by a peninsula and a reef. Within the harbor at Sumay was the U.S. Marine detachment and at Piti what little naval establishment we had on the island. Just a few miles north is Agana Bay where the capital of the island, Agana, lies.

The southern two thirds of the island is somewhat rugged, with many high hills, the highest of which is Mt. Lamlan, which

64

is almost as high as Mt. Topatchau on Saipan. Those hills are somewhat barren in appearance, though the valleys are well-watered and are heavily wooded.

The northern third of the island, which is our primary concern, is mainly a plateau from 300 to 600 feet high. No streams exist here, and both the east and west coasts of this portion of the island are abrupt and consist of bluffs and headlands. Coral reefs fringe much of the coast.

Today we are in nearly the same latitude as Guam, which is a possible forewarning of the climate there. The travel books say it is "agreeable and healthful" but you can judge for yourself. There are two seasons, "wet" and "dry", which describe themselves. From July to November is the rainy season with thundershowers concentrating in August, September and October brought by the monsoon. Typhoons may be expected in the vicinity from July through November also. Usually they are near misses and it is only about once in two years that one strikes the islands with the full force of cyclonic winds and torrential driving rains. Earthquakes are sometimes felt too.

Whether at sea or on the beach it is advisable to keep a "weather eye" open during the typhoon season. They go 150 miles per hour. At the first indication of a real typhoon it is advisable to secure all gear. The real danger seems to lie in wind-borne objects. The lee side of a cliff is a good protective shelter. The wind sometimes reverses its direction completely however. An even greater danger would be to be caught offshore in a small boat. The swells are terrific.

Amen! until tomorrow.

Tell Me More   July 15, 1944

Now that we have covered the physical characteristics of our target, let's see what man has done with God's handiwork. Guam was discovered by Magellan in 1521, Christianized in

1668 and remained under Spanish rule until 1898. At the close of the Spanish-American War it became a U.S. possession. The rest of the Marianas were sold to Germany, who in turn lost them to the Allies in World War I. Japan received them as a mandate for her share in that war.

In 1898, President McKinley placed the island of Guam under the control of the Navy Department. Therefore the Commandant of the Naval Station also headed the government of the island. Guam was occupied by the Japanese on December 10, 1941. The enemy task force consisted of three cruisers, three destroyers, and a convoy of eight merchant ships. Installations were bombed by the Saipan or Tinian Air Force and landings were made at Agana and Port Merizo by Naval Special Landing parties in conjunction with the army. Little damage was done and all Americans, military and civilian were captured.

Our defenses at that time consisted of some five concrete gun mounts, without guns (they were removed by the Washington Naval Treaty), 3-three inch AA guns on the U.S.S. *Penquin* and 2-fifty caliber AA machine-guns on the U.S.S. *R. L. Barnes*. The U.S. Marine Corps Detachment of about 160 men had some machine guns but no mobile artillery.

The total population of Guam in the 1940 census was 22,290. The natives are called Chamorros. Unlike the civilians on Saipan, these people are American nationals, who will undoubtedly welcome us. Most of them speak English and their religion is Catholic.

The origin of the ancient Chamorros is obscure. Originally they were probably Malayans but during the Spanish conquest between 1670-1696, these chocolate-colored aboriginals strenuously opposed Spanish domination. It was because of this that the Spaniards used such harsh methods in putting them down, many being killed and others leaving the islands. Because nearly all the native men were killed, the Spanish, Mexican and Filipino troops who garrisoned the island, took native wives. Therefore the Chamorros are a mixture of these bloods. Their language is also a mixture of native and Spanish lingo.

Guam has three classes of society. The upperclass owns the land and business establishments. Most of them are descendants of the old Spanish aristocracy. The middle class consists of shopkeepers, small ranchers and craftsmen. The lower class people are peaceful, good-natured, and law-abiding.

The Chamorros are submissive and probably not actively opposed to the Japanese. In other words, we cannot count on anything like the French underground to help us. There is little doubt that they will welcome American reoccupation of the island.

For the most part these people live in the capital, Agana, whose population was 10,000, and in eight towns with over 500 people. Agana itself is an interesting mixture of palm-thatched native houses, heavy stone, Spanish buildings, and now, bright, and modern American structures. It has all the modern conveniences of the ordinary American town, together with simpler structures and methods of an earlier day. Liberty is not highly recommended, however.

Economically the island has produced coconuts, rice, sugar, coffee and cocoa, and the U.S. Department of Agriculture has added many new products. Corn, sweet potatoes, bananas, pineapples, citrus fruits, limes, mangoes, tobacco, etc. have all been introduced and normally exported. About seventy percent of the island is forested and some timber is produced. Both cattle and water buffalo are raised. There are some wild deer, hogs and goats and ordinarily fishing is plentiful. Of course, Guam was also a coaling and cable station before the war.

Amen! until tomorrow.

The Marshalls   **July 16, 1944**

Yesterday we had contact with a friendly sub and today a tanker was sighted heading the other way. In between times we were passing by the Marshall Islands, outer bastion of the Japanese defense lines. The nearest we came to them was thirty-five miles today from Pikinni on the port side. Eniwetok lies on the western edge.

The Marshalls are characterized by thirty-two atolls — a great island-dotted reef surrounding a large inner lagoon. Most of them are widely separated, extending in two parallel chains about 700 miles in length. The western chain is called the Ralik, or sunset, Chain and the eastern, is the Radak, or Sunrise, Chain. Four islands of the Radak chain are still occupied by the enemy, though with supplies and communications cut off they must be in a near state of starvation at present.

These atolls vary greatly in size, most of them being quite large. The islands themselves are just slight elevations of coral and sand with a few coconut palms and shrubs here and there. Topsoil, or what there is of it, comes from decay of vegetation. There are some bananas, yams, breadfruit trees and taro and the lagoons generally are filled with fish. There is scarcely anything romantic or inviting about them.

In 1935 the population of all the Marshalls was said to be 481 Japanese and about 10,000 natives. The most populous was Majuro. We are fortunate in one way. Highest temperature here is in January and the lowest in July.

The people are Micronesian hybrids, brown in color and of good physique and comparatively high mentalities. They are good agriculturists, build some good boats and are remarkably good navigators. Their navigation "charts" are strips of wood bound together with fibers. Some of these show the positions of and distances between the islands. Their wooden canoes carry sails.

Coxswain "Pop" Robinson says, that to keep our record straight, the "Fort Funston" in Kansas should be Camp Funston. It was here, Pop says, that the 89th Division trained in the last war and maybe that is why we have the number 89.

                              Amen! until tomorrow.

After a Cook's tour of Eniwetok in a jeep here is the report I submit for your information. On the basis of this data perhaps you can answer the ever-popular question, "Would that be a good place for shore duty?"

Our amphibious forces landed on this atoll last February 17th but the last Japanese was not killed until about a month later. That doesn't mean that the fighting continued that long, in fact it was a rather short engagement, but it happened this way. A Marine challenged a sailor one night for identification. The sailor answered "I'm a CB." "Well, who is that behind you," persisted the Marine. "There is no one with me," answered the CB. At that the other "sailor" started to run. The Marine called for him to stop and then fired, wounding him in the leg. He got as far as the air strip when a second bullet stopped him permanently. The Japanese was in new Navy dungarees and had been living off pilfered stores and clothes that he obtained at night.

The rest of Tojo's buddies had already served a useful purpose. Eleven hundred were buried under the airstrip with tons of coral dropped on top of them to make a smooth runway for the fighters and bombers. The airstrip itself is the most important part of the island.

The men live mainly in tents though these are now to be replaced with Quonset huts. Their main problem is an adequate supply of water. All those little windmills you saw operating as we came into the lagoon yesterday, are homemade washing machines. They are to be seen everywhere in various shapes and sizes. The same can be said for the flies, though the clearing out of the underbrush has reduced their numbers.

For recreation the men swim in beautiful clear water and do some fishing. The beaches are mostly good. A recreation center is being built at one of them. The officers have a club on the north end of the island. There are several large outdoor movies and ball diamonds. The mail service is reported good with six days from the east coast not unusual. There are three very cleverly constructed chapels throughout the island, built and designed by the CBs.

What has happened to the natives? You remember I previously reported their number at about 120 as of several years ago. Our occupying forces found only 80, these mostly old men and women and children. They told us that each year the Japanese authorities would take away the young men and women, supposedly to forced labor on other islands. The eighty Marshallese were removed to another island where they live to themselves, supplied with necessities by Uncle Sam. Some were first cared for in our hospitals.

And here I am on that seemingly inexhaustive subject, our namesake. It would be much easier to have bought a book on the General, if any have been written. Anyway I have a clipping now from a Honolulu paper announcing the meeting of the General Frederick Funston Post of the V. F. W. Also there is pretty good reason to believe that the General had much to do with the relief of San Francisco during the great earthquake and fire of 1906.

Amen! until tomorrow.

The Plan   **July 19, 1944**

As you already know, Guam is U.S. territory in Japanese hands and is of considerable strategic importance. What is this strategic value? It has two airstrips, a seaplane base and a harbor. Its large area (twice the size of Saipan) offers sites for large airfields. The Apra Harbor can be developed into a medium or first class base. Because of these factors Guam will be an important step in helping to sever the enemies supply line to the south as well as provide an advanced staging area for future operations. In other words we will be making of Guam the fortress and naval base that it should have been before December 1941.

Since our first drives will be directed to securing Apra Harbor and surrounding area we will become most familiar with its characteristics. Lying on the south-west side, it is the only good harbor on Guam. The enemy is using it for a refueling and supply base but, as far as it is known, not as a fleet anchorage. The harbor is formed by tiny Cabras Island and reef with breakwater, on its north side. On the southern border of the harbor is the important finger of land called Orote Peninsula. The best airfield is located here. It has a single strip approximately 6,000 feet long. One picture shows about thirty aircraft on this strip.

Prior to December 1941 there was no airfield on Guam. Besides Orote the Japanese now have constructed one near the town of Agana and also had under construction two others in the northern portion of the island.

Beaches favor the defense, due to the 25-700 yard wide reef that virtually surrounds the island, and the high cliffs above most beaches. Small bays and harbors backed by rolling country, offer suitable landing points, for men and material. The most suitable beaches for a landing force are in the area between Facpi Point and Alupat Island in the Apra Harbor area.

"There are several plans for attack, and since we are a reserve outfit we have to be ready to fit into any one of them on short notice," according to Col. Learner. The most likely plan is that the 3rd Marine Division will land at Asan. The 1st Brigade, together with the 305th Regiment of the 77th Division, will land at Agat. The two divisions will then move to pincer off Apra Harbor. Of vital importance will be to secure the ridge overlooking the beaches so that the same thing will not occur to our beaches here as occurred at Saipan. Once the ridge is secured and the units have merged, the clearing out of Orote peninsula will begin.

If you have been listening carefully to the news you have probably noticed what a terrific pounding Guam and Tinian have been undergoing since July 8th. Not only our fleet units of battleships, cruisers, destroyers and carriers have been pouring in shells and bombs but this time land-based planes from

Isley field on Saipan, carrying heavier loads than a carrier plane, are adding strength to strength. After all it is only 121 miles from Apra Harbor to Garapan. When you remember that the real softening up of Saipan did not begin until D-3, it gives you a good idea of just what an advantage this has.

William Day or D day is Friday on Guam and soon after on Tinian. We will arrive on Saturday and probably unload on that day or Sunday. It is still unknown whether this outfit will go in after the Marines at Agat or Asan or on some new beach.

This morning the convoy was practicing emergency turns and finally ended up making a complete circle within the escort. If Willy is on our stern he will have a hard time following that maneuver.

Amen! until tomorrow.

Operation: Medical   July 20, 1944

Ellison E. Gilbert, CM2c, became the center of the careful attention today of two ships in the convoy only two days from their target objective and within reach of enemy submarines. None of us knew this young sailor but from the attention he got he could have been a crown prince. The care with which the Destroyer Escort *Elden* drew along our port side, the skill with which the deck force lowered the Salmon Board to the deck of the *Elden* and then hoisted the patient safely across to our deck made the whole operation look too easy. It was a skillfully executed transfer and deserves a hearty "well-done."

You will be glad to know that Ellison was operated on for acute appendicitis shortly after he arrived aboard and is now resting nicely.

There are a few matters in regard to our objective that have been overlooked. If you survive the shrapnel, bullets and steel of the enemy you may be interested in preserving your health on this tropical island.

Generally sanitary conditions on Guam are only fair. The standard of living of the natives was low, towns were over-crowded and there was lack of personal sanitations. Sewage facilities at Agana were considered adequate though in villages and rural areas the facilities were considered primitive. But regardless of the adequacy of sewage facilities, a bombard-ment of the place will effect such wreckage of precautionary health measures as to delight swarms of flies and insects which are ever ready to feast upon pollution. Experience of other campaigns have proved that it is absolutely necessary to ob-serve every sanitary measure possible in order to avoid the ter-rible rigors of dysentery: Keep flies off your food. Don't drink untreated ground water. Don't eat raw or unwashed vegeta-bles or fruits unless you can peel them. Wash your hands be-fore eating, whenever possible.

In addition to the annoyance of flies, there will be fleas, mosquitoes, centipedes and scorpions. Dengue fever is carried by mosquitoes; and also dysentery, typhoid fever, paratyphoid and some eye, skin and venereal diseases are prevalent.

The natives know the natural hazards and it will be well for you to note the following, since coral is a special feature of Guam and especially around Orote Peninsula. Holes in coral have razor edges. Coral cuts can be brutally painful so keep those G.I. shoes handy. On the southern half of the island there is another disagreeable item in sword (or saw) grass. This usually grows about chest high and can give a very nasty cut.

If you get a chance later to go fishing or swimming you will want to remember that deep water fish are edible but fish living in shallow flats along shore are not. There are sea crabs that are edible but all sea food spoils quickly. On land there is a small grey crab that is considered poisonous and a coco-nut crab, with brown belly and large claws that is edible.

In 1938 Chief Commissary Steward Smith visited Guam and one of his shipmates composed the following poem, which, though not quite applicable to our situation, might by of interest to you:

When I first came to Agana,
They bedecked me with flowers so gay,
But I wish they'd been placed on my coffin
For then I'd be going away.

For Guam is the land where the earth quakes
And Guam is the land where it's hot
And Guam is the land where the bugs are
It's the land the good Lord forgot.

If I had the wings of a carabee
I'd go to the Governor and say
"I'm leaving this island tomorrow
For there's a ship that's sailing today."

To go over the hill from Agana
Is a cinch topographically
There are plenty of hills to go over
But beyond each darn hill lies the sea.

'Tis the end of my sad lamentation
"That poor nut is balmy," you say.
Maybe so, but Guam will sure get you
And soon you'll be the same way.

Amen! until tomorrow.

William Day   **July 21, 1944**

Because this was D day on Guam our thoughts are naturally there but there is no further news to add to what you heard this afternoon. The news is better than just good but it is still early to really tell whether all the Japanese are commiting hari-kari or whether their defenses have yet to be really encountered.

In all, our estimates give them 17,673 Army troops, 2,185 air personnel, 3,375 combatant navy troops, 4,888 Japanese CB's, and an estimated 8,100 reinforcements bringing their total strength to 36,218.

In the main the enemy seems to have defended the area from Tumon Bay to Agat, the heaviest. The Marines struck within this area. The list of their heavy and light weapons is too long to repeat. The bombardment should have taken care of most of the coastal emplacements and shore batteries. But the enemy also appear to have a large amount of mobile artillery and mortars as well as reserve battalions which can cause difficulty for some time even after the beachheads are secure.

I mentioned the other night that the natives will be friendly but will probably be of little aid to the actual fighting. I have since been informed that we had trained 150 native Guards and 250 naval insular forces as well as thirty USN medical corps nurses. They should be of great help if they are still there.

Since it won't be long until we will land you on the beaches of Guam, we would like to say now that we hope this trip has not been too tough. Conditions were more crowded than we have known for some time. It meant a strain on the patience at times and a cramping of the muscles. But we did our best for you. Once we land you on the beach, our responsibility is at an end and you're on your own. We say to you as we have to other outfits, that if you do your share once you get there, the Navy will be only too glad to take you home or to a rest camp, when you say the word.

It is our custom on the night before an invasion to ask you to uncover and stand fast where you are while we direct our thoughts to Almighty God for a moment.

Almighty God, who art the creator and sustainer of all men, grant thy grace unto us that we may endeavor in good faith to win a righteous victory, not only for ourselves, but for our loved ones, for our country, and for those who believe in the cause of freedom everywhere.

Fill us with wisdom to meet any difficulty and gird
us with the strength to meet any peril. To the end that
we may do our duty in the eyes of men and for Thee.
Amen.

Amen! until tomorrow.

W plus 1   July 22, 1944

As Col. Learner has related, things are going mighty well
on the beach. The Marines are pushing right ahead. The results
of the aerial and naval bombardment are evident everywhere
and for the satisfaction of all hands, Japanese dead are all over
the beach areas, greatly outnumbering the dead Marines.

On the Agat beach there was a strong battery of artillery
and network of caves dug into the hill. From those batteries
a control vessel and SC had been sunk and an LCI hit. Either
a destroyer or heavy demolition charges had blown this battery to pieces.

If you will remember back to D day on Saipan you will
recall that Guam was to be invaded by the 3rd Marines on D
plus 3. You have probably wondered where they have been
since then. For fifty-three days these troops were aboardship,
plying the Pacific. No wonder they went to town when they
hit the beach! Another suggested reason is that the beach itself is not very inviting and they pushed in fast to get away
from its smell and tropical vegetation. Anyway they are pushing, thankfully against resistance not as tough as Saipan. There
is no artillery barrage on the beach.

We are headed out to sea tonight and will be out tomorrow or until such time as we are needed. You have asked about
the lashing of the life rafts together on the boat deck. This
is one way of getting across the reefs and mud on this beach
if LVT's and ducks are not available.

Amen! until tomorrow.

By this time it is possible to get a general picture of the action on Guam over a period of one week. Piecing together the radio news and the experiences of our casualties here is what comes out.

The Japanese expected the landings on the beaches of Asan and Agat and they were not wrong. The bombardment of seventeen days had done its work in knocking out gun emplacements and installations but the beaches and reefs had also been fortified with anti-boat impalements and barbed wire. It was a naval demolition squad that took care of these. The landings were made without great casualties and the two units moved toward each other, while holding down their flanks. There were "banzai" counter attacks the first few days and several tanks were knocked out on the Harmon road.

By the time the end of the peninsula was reached the jungle was so thick only a few yards ahead could be seen. Here Marines and Japanese fought it out, yelling at each other through the jungle. Favorite war cry of the Japanese was, "Marine, you die!" The return cry of the Marines could hardly be repeated. Snipers were everywhere and you were just as likely to find one in back of you as in front. Very few prisoners were taken. The only two known captured were a major, whose good English saved him and an American-born Japanese with him.

The going was tough in there, the brunt of the push up the peninsula being carried by the 22nd Marines and a regiment of the 4th Division. Japanese fanatical charges helped them considerably. After one charge the Japanese were found piled three deep. Some went down the cliff and tried to swim around behind our lines. They were spotted and picked off. It appeared that some of the troops were poorly clad and armed while others had new equipment. One unit of Imperial Marines was guarding the airfield. It is not likely that any of them will escape.

The captured Japanese gave details of how the enemy had planned to defend the island. All natives in the northern portion of the island had been herded into a concentration camp on the eastern side. They were not allowed anyplace near installations. Some escaped to tell the tale of their hardships.

Souvenirs seemed to have been plentiful judging from the stuff some of the casualties brought aboard. There are four samurai swords, three of which can be seen in my office, and numerous gadgets. On the word of two eye-witnesses we have heard that the Japanese officer's sword is not just an ornament but is actually swung into action with one or two hands on occasion.

Our casualties aboard number 144 of which 116 are Marines, nineteen are army and nine are Navy. Four officers are among them. Of the Navy casualties, five are from our own ship's company. They are Lt. (jg) Downey, A. Depasquale, Green, E. H. Prosser and Jensen. All were only slightly wounded. In fact our patients as a whole are in better shape than the casualties from Saipan. We have seventy-seven ambulatory cases and sixty-seven bed patients, no amputations and no deaths.

It may have seemed that this action was the easiest of the *Funston's* four invasions. In spite of that however, all hands did a 4.0 job. It was tough beach to unload on and the boat division and the thirty hand working party deserve special mention for their fine work. I took one trip to the reef and I want to say that it makes you proud of your ship to see the efficient manner in which the boat coxswains handled their craft, as well as the smart appearance of our boats. While other boats were setting around waiting to be unloaded, we did the job ourselves and were the first ship 100 percent unloaded. Everyone deserves a feeling of pride over that.

Amen! until tomorrow.

Leyte, P.I.

A compilation of broadcasts to ship's personnel and troops on board U.S.S. Frederick Funston (APA-89)

What Again?   September 15, 1944

Already the *Funston* and the 96th Division have had a chance to become acquainted at Maui. Now that we are shipmates how about a little more information about each other. The 96th is out to make its niche in history. In the first World War the Division never got overseas. Existing as a paper organization after the war it was re-formed August 16th, 1942. On July 28th, just a month and a half ago, they arrived in Hawaii. The division insignia has not been worn in Hawaii and few of us have ever seen it. It consists of a blue diamond superimposed on a white diamond, the colors standing for fidelity and purity. Most of the man are from the midwest with a sprinkling of "you-alls" and bowlegs thrown in for good measure. The division has a high rating in their training, being one of the few outfits that has never had to take re-tests on their training problems. You look good to us fellows and we wish you the best of luck as you head for your first pay-run.

Many of the troops are already familiar with the name *Funston*, having lived on a street and passed through a gate bearing the same name at Schofield Barracks. It is a worthy name of a great general and a worthy ship. We are proud of her. Comissioned by the Navy in April 1943, she was built in Tacoma, Washington, and made one trip to Guadalcanal and Australia as an Army transport before the Navy took her over. Officially we are known as APA-89, an auxiliary, a transport of the combat type, that is, we carry boats for beach landings which distinguishes us from other transports.

Amen! until tomorrow.

Ziggin' and Zaggin'   September 16, 1944

You have probably wondered what all this seemingly silly zig zaggin is for. No, it is not to exercise the helmsmen. It is all a part of the game to outsmart the opponents. Our coach is on the *Rocky Mount*. Our quarterback is on the *Cambria*. He decides what particular pattern the team will use. Every little while the entire formation changed from one pattern to another, like the Notre Dame football team shifting after a huddle. It is fascinating to watch the entire convoy moving in unison, zigzagging constantly. Of course there is always the possibility of collision through error on someone's part. The ships endeavor to keep in exact formation however, because our escort protection is organized on the basis of our keeping position. If one ship gets out of line, it endangers the entire convoy. In a way it is like a football player getting offside and thereby penalizing his whole team.

Some of you may have noticed another convoy running interference for us on the horizon. It seems to be about the same size as our own with the addition of two escort carriers, which are always good to have around. Probably it is the veteran 7th Army Division in our same task unit.

With tonight's broadcast we institute three contests for all hands on board. Prizes of two cartons of cigarettes or $1 in ship's store trade will be given to the winners of the best article of about 100 words on the subject "What I Am Fighting For"; to the best original poem on any subject; and the best cartoon on any subject. Sign your name, rank, and outfit on them and leave them at the library or chaplain's office before 2000 next Wednesday night. The winning poem and article will be read over this broadcast in the near future.

Amen! until tomorrow.

One We Missed   **September 17, 1944**

Since the war in the Palau Islands is rapidly becoming nearer to us than the war in Europe, let's turn our attention to there tonight. The first landings were made on Peleliu Island

and the news today reveals a surprise landing on Anguar. This operation is being carried out by the 81st Army Division and the 1st Marine Division, the former outfit getting it's "baptism of fire." Incidentally our sister ship, the U.S.S. *James O'Hara* (APA90), is in on this operation.

At one time I spoke of the Japanese holdings in the Pacific as like a great two-edged axe blade, the handle being swung in Tokyo. One edge of the axe is the Marshall Islands that we are approaching. Until they were eliminated they had done plenty of damage to Pearl Harbor and convoys. The other side of the axe blade is 2,500 miles away. It consists of the Palau (or Pelew) Islands and neighboring groups. From here the Philippines are only 600 miles away, less than the distance from New York to Chicago, and the same distance from Gen. MacArthur's landings in Morotai.

Palau is Japan's Singapore. It's more than 100 islands barricade a magnificent fleet base. It is the headquarters of the entire Japanese South Seas government. Officials and officers so swarmed there that visitors, of which there have been only about a dozen, do not draw a breath without an appropriate note being made in the archives.

In 1934 the census listed 10,600 people on these islands of which about one-half were Japanese. However, immigrants from Nippon have poured ashore with such a fever of activity in the past five years that towns were leaping up and the native Kanakas were being forced into interior forests. Industries were being developed and agriculture promoted to add to the few chickens, pigs and fish available. Thatched huts have disappeared.

Of course the purpose was to make the island stronghold self-contained and self-supporting in case of a siege such as they are now undergoing. Ship basins were being dredged deeper, channels widened, islands leveled to provide airdromes. Just a short time ago both planes and ships were providing regular service to the Philippines, New Guinea and Nippon.

To give you an idea of how the army and Marines are operating there, here is the situation. Peleliu is the southernmost island of a group of islands bound by exceptionally large reefs.

On two sides the reefs extend seventy-seven miles. It is wooded. The troops have established a battle line across a two mile wide portion. Fighting here has been tough in places with the Japanese making several tank-led counter-attacks. Maj. Gen. Julian Smith said, "The situation is more completely satisfactory, we have advantage and complete control of the air."

Angaur, where Marines and Army made the recent landing, is separated to the south from these other islands by a 5½ miles channel. It has a harbor and a village of 1,000 people on the west side named, prophetically perhaps, Saipan. Initial objectives were quickly obtained and troops are advancing inland from the secured beachhead.

Amen! until tomorrow.

Talent Wanted   September 18, 1944

The convoy underwent a simulated air attack this afternoon from carrier based aircraft. Judging from the word from the admiral the attack was successfully repelled, we hope.

It has been proposed that we see how much talent there is aboard and put on a "smokeless" smoker on top of No. 4 hatch before we reach Eniwetok. Whether we have it or not depends on your response. So here goes for try-outs. All hands who sing, play an instrument, impersonate, dance, make with the jive or anything else that comes under the heading of entertainment, will please lay down to the starboard side of the wardroom at 2000 tonight.

Amen! until tomorrow.

You have all heard of the Caterpillar Club, the Short-Snorter Club and Scooterpoopers Club. Well, in seafaring life we have three such semi-official organizations. There is the Shellback Club for all men who have crossed the equator; The Polar Bear Club for all who have crossed the Arctic or Antarctic circles. Tomorrow morning about 0900 we will leave the occidental world and enter into the mysteries of the Orient. When you feel the bump we will have crossed that mysterious enigma, the International Date Line at the 180th meridian. Automatically you will all become members of the Imperial Domain of the Golden Dragon and will be known henceforth as Dragonbacks. We will make that official tomorrow night.

The International Date Line is only a few degrees from the Marshall Islands, first Oriental and enemy territory we will pass through. To introduce you to this new world we will start with a poem tonight entitled, "Stepping Stones to Japan",

The islands like Kwajalein, Saipan, and Wake,
Or Tarawa, Marcus, and Yap
Sound funny or queer to American troops
When they look them up on a map.

There's Engibi, Rota, and Bonins and Truk,
Majuro, Namur, and Palau,
Formosa, Kusaie, Eniwetok, and Roi,
Plus Ponape, Guam, and Davae.

These tongue-twisting, weird, unpronounceable spots
Point the way that our forces will go
Through the skies, on the seas, over mountains and plains
To knock out our Nipponese foe.

Anyone is bound to wonder where all this hodge-podge of names came from, especially when some islands have two names. Who were Gilbert and Marshall anyway? Actually no one paid much attention to these islands until recently. Now some of their interesting history is being collected. Here is what we have found.

85

Magellan, the first European to cross the Pacific, managed to miss every island between the straits and Guam. Then Garcia de Loyasa was sent out to follow up Magellan's discoveries in 1525. He just missed the Marshalls by two degrees. So the discoveries waited for two obscure English seamen, not otherwise known to fame, who have left their names on the Gilberts and Marshalls.

Their vessels, the *Charlotte* and *Scarborough* were merchant ships chartered to carry 334 convicts to Australia with a Royal Marine guard and the marine's wives. After discharging their unwilling cargo, Marshall, the master of the *Scarborough* and Gilbert, master of the *Charlotte* sailed for Canton. This was 1788. Looks like pretty poor navigation but supposedly, in order to avoid the Torres Strait and Molucca pirates, they went on a wide sweep to the north and discovered both the Gilberts and Marshalls.

Amen! until tomorrow.

A Friend Passes: Autumn Arrives
September 21, 1944

On Saturday at 1430 and Sunday 1430 the grand "smokeless-smoker" will be held on top No. 4. Advance information has it that the show is so good, the Eniwetok Grand Opera House has asked for a performance. Main feature will be a troupe of vivacious females, presumably flown out from Dorothy Lamour's tropical paradise.

We were all sorry to hear of the loss of the U.S.S. *Noa* (APD-24). It was on June 13th that this bobbing, green boat heaved to along our port side and received not only fuel but our ice cream, books and bread. It seems her bake ovens broke down. She had an impressive list of battle flags on her bridge. Now after twenty-three years of service she has seen her last fight and we have lost a personal acquaintance.

Getting back to our own little world, it has become evident that we will pass through the northernmost island of the Marshalls. There are thirty-four of these low-lying atolls and single islands, arranged roughly in two parallel chains, the first being the Radak Chain and the second the Ralik Chain. All together they cover an area one and one-half the size of Texas but their actual land area is only seventy-four square miles, 1/20th the size of Rhode Island.

Most important to us is the largest atoll in the world, Kwajalein, and Eniwetok. However, four on this side are still occupied by the Japanese. They are Wotje, Maloelap, Jaluit and Mili. Constantly pounded and with their supply lines cut off for many months, they are a lot easier to take care of as they are, than to risking lives to take them.

Around the last named, Mili atoll, an incident took place in 1824 that was reported in the Boston papers as a "horrid affair". It seems the crew of the whaling ship *Nantucket* mutinied and murdered the master and mates. They then took her into Mille lagoon with the intention of settling down on the atoll, but quarrelled over the loot and the women, hanged the steward, and shot the chief mutineer — a New Yorker, as the Boston papers hastened to add. Meanwhile a few men and boys left aboard the ship, cut her cables, made sail and escaped, saving both the ship and their necks.

Another event of this group is worth mentioning. On December 14, 1816 the *Rurik* sailed from "Hana-ruru" (Honolulu to you) with a crew of Russians and scientists. At Wotje they stayed for quite a while and became friendly with the natives. The natives were building thirty-eight foot canoes with primitive tools. The Russian leader, Kotzebue, describes the women as very beautiful and although "seemingly modest, a bit of iron sufficed to make these savage beauties succumb." Maybe Dorothy Lamour wasn't so far off after all, only she was 125 years too late.

Today is the 21st day of September. If you have felt those cool breezes, a nip in the air and smelled burning leaves, it is all because tomorrow is the first day of autumn, no fooling.

At this time of year the sun is right smack-dab over the equator and headed "down under."

Amen! until tomorrow.

The Winners   September 22, 1944

Few incidents have occurred on this trip thus far but the ones that have should be like "handwriting on the wall." A couple of days ago the APD *Humphries* reported a solid contact but no depth charges were dropped. Last night a red alert was held at Eniwetok. These are warnings that Japanese reconnaisance may be feeling us out, waiting the right opportunity to harass our far flung lines in the Western Pacific.

The third incident occurred last night when a hoist call from Burnside six in the convoy ahead of us announced a "man overboard." This was at 0230. Immediately two escorts were ordered to "operate independently to recover the man." Our convoy manuevered out of the way. A second order was given, "you cowboys use illumination necessary to recover the man." (The cowboys are the escorts who ride herd on us.) The search was unsuccessful. At dawn planes were sent out to continue the search but no results were reported. This is a second warning to us. It isn't necessary to have a rough sea to lose a man overboard. He could have been climbing around where he didn't belong looking for a cool place to sleep. He could have been sitting on the rail or leaned too far over. At any rate watch your step and keep that lifebelt handy.

The judges have announced the winners from the thirty-three entries in the ship's contest. Out of fifteen entries in the "Why I Am Fighting" contest the judges gave second place to S/Sgt. Norman Drunn, 593rd JASCO. First place went to Pvt. Robert Boucher, Anti-Tank Co., 382nd. Out of eleven entries in the poetry contest, second place went to Robert McGowan, MoMM2c, ship's company, with a poem entitled

"An Ardent Desire." First place went to S/Sgt. Sands, Co. "M", 382nd, with a poem entitled, "The Lady of Tomorrow." There were seven entries in the cartoon contest. Second place went to R. L. Rossi, SClc, ship's company, and first place to John J. Archibald, 96th Recon. Troop. The winning cartoons will be under the counter in the library tomorrow for display.

Here is the winning article, "Why I Am Fighting!" by Pvt. Robert Boucher:

> *I'm fighting for a son and daughter; they are not yet born but they will be. They want a home, a yard to play in, movies to see, free school to attend, and pop and ice cream to eat. I'm fighting also, to say, "No, I won't!" and have someone weigh my reasons. I'm fighting for the chance to say, "I'm a Democrat, so what!" Above all though, I'm fighting for an altar where I can kneel in peace and quiet and say, "My Lord and God, I love you."*

Prizes will be presented to the winners at tomorrow's smoker. The smoker will begin at 1400 on top No. 4 hatch for all men in holds 4 and 5 and promenade decks. All others will attend the Sunday show. Ship's company may attend either performance.

Amen! until tomorrow.

Queen Of Battle   September 23, 1944

It was Ernie Pyle that said, "I believe you could take any thousand soldiers in our armed services, and out of them create a show." And what a show we had this afternoon! There was genuine talent and despite the heat and occasional interruptions everyone appreciated it. Tomorrow the same show will be given at 1400 for all men who did not see the one today.

Here is the prize-winning poem written by S/Sgt. Sands of "M" Company. It is titled "The Lady of Tomorrow":

The "Queen of Battle" is yet a virgin,
To test her strength against the Jap,
And teach to them the modern version,
Of what it means to be set back.

The men who'll fight for this proud Queen,
Are out to win for her a throne.
A throne that represents their dream
Of everlasting peace at home.

This Queen, by now a lady fair,
Who in her early years of life.
Was never given the chance to bear,
The edge of battle on her knife.

But now the Queen, with tested men,
Straps on a knife with diamond edge.
And leads the way to world's end,
To conquer injustice, is her one pledge.

With her job done and homeward bent
Her thoughts on her own happiness.
She'll never dream of the extent
Of joy to all the world she'll bless.

The famous report of the submarine U.S.S. *Sturgeon* when she returned from her first kill was, "Sturgeon no longer virgin." In another month the 96th can say the same.

A message was received today for all ships:

To Admiral W. F. Halsey: "You are living up to your reputation for smacking the Japanese. The Navy Department is proud of the latest exploit of the third fleet. I send my congratulations to you and to Vice Adm. Mitscher and his carrier force and to all the ships and men who participated in this successful operation." Signed James Forrestal. The message was relayed to us as part of Adm. Halsey's command.

We are well into the Marshalls tonight. The closest we will come to any of them is seventeen miles from Taka or Suverov atoll at 1900 tonight. The largest atoll in the world, Kwajalein, which was the first of the Marshalls to be occupied by our forces from January 31st to February 6th of this year, is sixty miles to the south of our course. It was discovered by Captain Mertho of the British ship *Ocean* in 1804. There is a strong air base there and it is a staging area for operations. It is a stop on the air route from Pearl Harbor to the Marianas; planes hop from Johnston to Kwajalein to Eniwetok to Saipan or Guam.

It is well to take a moment here to explain what an atoll is. Simply speaking the difference between an atoll and an island is that the former is coral reef around a body of water whereas the latter is a piece of land with water all around it. The islands of the north and west Pacific are for the most part of volcanic origin and are in varying stages of development. Here are the four stages these volcanos go through to give birth to an atoll.

First a volcano pushes up from the bottom floor. Second the volcano erupts, thrusting itself above sea level. Thirdly, the volcano quiets down and starts to sink, a fringe of coral reef forms on its shoulders. Fourth, still sinking the mountain supports a barrier reef with a lagoon between the island and the reef. Lastly the mountain sinks and only the rim of the reef remains, a typical Pacific atoll.

Amen! until tomorrow.

We Raise Our Sights   September 28, 1944

Never a dull moment on the *Funston*. Who said, "There is nothing new under the sun"? Actually so many changes have taken place since we left Honolulu most of us have been lost trying to piece the puzzle together. Perhaps if I take up the situation step by step you can get it together.

1. Our original target was Yap Island, a strong base in the western Carolines and 275 miles north of Palau, and Ulithi. While we have been at sea the Yap base was neutralized by Vice Adm. Mitscher's carrier force. Furthermore, landings were made without opposition on Ulithi, an atoll 120 miles farther to the northeast. No opposition was encountered because the entire Japanese garrison had withdrawn.

2. Secondly, Mitscher's carriers and Adm. Halsey's Third Fleet began dishing out their knockout punches to the southern Philippines, especially the large island of Mindanao. They have destroyed several hundred Japanese planes and sunk an entire convoy of thirty-two ships with negligible losses and little opposition. It was time for momentous decisions. Probably Adm. Halsey sent a message to Adm. Nimitz saying something like this, "Chet, this is Bill. Tell Mac he can get underway now." So the time schedule in the Western Pacific gets moved up a couple of months just like that and you and I will go beyond our original target to share in the great task of liberating the Philippines.

3. Thirdly, we must begin changing plans for our part in this great operation. First of all our staging area was changed. Since our 96th and 7th Divisions will serve under the great MacArthur himself, we must go down to his rendezvous. That is where we are headed now. Our course is 190⁰, nearly due south. Following along the eastern edge of the Caroline Islands we will later cut east and cross the equator at an angle, arriving at our staging area, Manus, about Tuesday morning. To do this we will have to thumb our nose at Japanese bases of Ponape and Kusaie, but I will tell you more of them tomorrow.

There have been a good many questions arise concerning the ratio of our time with the states. Tonight I want to give it to you straight and if you want to write it down and make changes as our clocks change you will always be able to say what time it is in Eyewash. When it is 1800 Eniwetok time it is 0300 in New York the same day, 0200 in Chicago, 0100 in Denver and Los Angeles, midnight between yesterday and today in San Francisco, and 2130 yesterday in Honolulu.

From the looks of things it seems likely that we will be out this way for some time. Therefore may I remind you to take special care of such non-replaceable items as books, magazines, games and such. That goes for the crew as well as the troops. The day may come when a September magazine will look as new as this morning's newspaper.

Amen! until tomorrow.

Storm Warning   September 29, 1944

Hear Ye! Hear Ye! Hear Ye!

All persons laying claim to be Shellbacks must appear before the Aide to His Majesty, Neptunas Rex, after general quarters in the officer's lounge.

All properly qualified Shellbacks will establish an organization to safeguard the royal domain of Neptune on the occasion of the passing of the U.S.S. *Frederick Funston* into that domain on or about October 1st, 1944, A.D.

All persons unable to qualify as Shellbacks will henceforth be known as Pollywogs until such time as they are summoned before the Royal Highness and shall thereby qualify for admission to the Royal Order of Trusty Shellbacks.

Signed: Davey Jones,
His Royal Scribe.

Behind the screen of rain and mist today we have been passing through the eastern islands of the Carolines. At 1700 we were ninety miles from the Japanese base of Kusaie off port beam and 200 miles from the big island of Ponape on starboard beam earlier in the day at 1400.

If you follow the axe handle from Tokyo through the Bonins and Marianas you realize that the Carolines constitute the broad head of the axe. Because of their strategic geographical position the Japanese developed them as advance naval, air,

93

and supply bases for their attempted conquest of New Guinea, the Bismarcks, the Solomons and Australia. Any north-south movement in the western Pacific is dominated by these islands. They are made up in forty-eight clusters of 600 islands that add up to 525 square miles. But spread out as they are 1,700 miles from east to west and 550 miles from north to south they occupy a space of 820,000 square miles, or an area one-fourth the size of the U.S.

These islands were discovered by the Spanish explorers of the 16th century but they were largely left undeveloped. In 1868 Spain named them "Carolines" in honor of their king, Charles II. Spanish Catholic and American Protestant missionaries have converted three-fifths of the natives to Christianity.

After the Spanish-American War we had an opportunity to take the Carolines over. We showed no interest and so Spain sold them to Germany. Germany developed the copra trade until 1915 when Japanese naval squadrons sailed in and took them over as a war prize, continuing to rule them under a mandate granted by the League of Nations.

Kusaie, Ponape and Truk are all of volcanic origin. Of these Ponape is the largest single island in the Japanese Mandate, and covers about 130 square miles. It has a large ship basin and six excellent harbors. Our strategy seems to have called for the neutralization of the large bases of Yap, Truk, Ponape and Kusaie. The fact that this has been accomplished through air and sea power is attested by our ability to sail so close to them. Naval PBY pilots at Eniwetok told us that in daily patrols to these latter two islands they have encountered no opposition and only occasionally some flak.

If we were attacking any of them in the eastern group, my guess would be that Ponape would have the honor. Out here this island is a crossroads, like Hawaii. The Spaniards made Ponape their headquarters. Even before then the natives regarded it as a crossroad for they are a blend of Polynesian, Melanesian, Malay and Japanese. It is so close to New Guinea that one tale has it that crocodiles are washed out to sea by

rivers and drift over. Their folklore tells of ancient Ponape-
ans venturing out so far they saw the eruption of Kilauea on
Hawaii. Their language shows similarities to that spoken in
Tahiti, Samoa and the Marquesas.

It is June around here all the year round. They don't know
anything about seasons. The temperature sticks around 80°F.
all the year round even though we are just a few degrees above
the equator. The rain reminds us that Kusaie is one of the
world's wettest spots with 225 inches annually. We are in the
hurricane belt and typoons may visit the area at any time. These
are what we knew as "twisters" back home. The wind last night
only got up to sixty miles per hour. This is called a "storm"
even though the gusts were irregular.

There are several stories about these people I want to tell
you tomorrow night but maybe I can slip one in tonight. The
hardy Ponapean is a tough guy. He sleeps on a wooden floor
and uses a wooden pillow. The Japanese offered him their
manufactured wooden pillow but he rejected it because the thin
cloth over the wood made it uncomfortably soft. He makes
his women do all his work while he makes war, or, when he
is not allowed to make it, he sits around and talks about it.

Amen! until tomorrow.

By Seaweed Telegraph　　　　　**September 30, 1944**

Hear Ye! Hear Ye! Hear Ye!

Following received by Seaweed Telegraph from Admiral
Davey Jones, Royal Scribe to his Imperial Majesty the Ruler
of the Raging Main:

> *Neptunus Rex greeting to Rear Admiral Forrest Royal,*
> *Senior Shellback of Task Group 33.2 and is pleased to*
> *see him reenter his kingdom. With my aids and staff I*
> *will board the ships under your command on the evening*

of October first to serve subjectona on such slimey scum
as may have the temerity of attempting to enter this realm
in the company of your honorable Shellbacks. Have your
ships ready to render me the full honor of my rank and
have all miserable Pollywogs ready to attend my wishes.
At 0900 local time on October second his Imperial
Majesty Neptunus Rex, Ruler of the Raging Main, and
Monarch of the Deep attended by his Royal Wife and
Royal Baby, his lawyers, doctors, scribes, polar bears,
bulls, mermaids, sea serpents, and a host of other crea-
tures of the briny deep will board the ships of your com-
mand to hear the pleas of such scum as may be about
to mete out injustice to all and to determine which, if
any, are fit to be permitted to enter his realm. Direct all
loyal and trusty Shellbacks of the Ancient Order of the
Deep that they shall be prepared to assist in the trial and
instructions of these backwater scum and a lousy miser-
able and presumptious Pollywog. Attend Ye all this
order.

Admiral Davey Jones.''

Ordinarily we think of these natives of Kusaie and Ponape as barbarians. However archeologists are puzzled by the massive stone structures found there. They consist of canals, walls and courts built of enormous stone which could be moved only by men with some knowledge of engineering. They are probably the remains of a Polynesian civilization of long ago.

Perhaps it was the white man that made the natives so warlike. It goes back to the old whaling days when they came into contact with the dredges of our people. Trade in firearms and whiskey for native products went on. Other American presents were venereal disease, small pox and a 100 other diseases that the natives had no resistance for. The population was reduced two-thirds in eighty years and the treatment of the natives was so bad the people rose and drove the whalers out. Not only that but Kusaie was the headquarters of the notorious Clevelander, "Bully Hayes," pirate head of the "Blackbirders." For twenty years they practiced the lowest form of kidnapping islanders for sale into slavery in Mexico and South America.

Fortunately for us their experience with Americans since the 1850s has changed all this. Their contact with decent, honorable men and the missionaries is all they now associate with the name American. As Williard Price said, "Americans damned the islands and Americans redeemed them." We might add, the job will have to be done over again now.

The Ponapean is an especially dangerous fellow to anyone who treats him unfairly. The Spaniards had to build a wall six feet thick surrounding a blockhouse to withstand him.

The young men slash their arms and burn holes in their breasts to show their contempt for pain. They have a weapon like a sling, and a native bow taller than a man. Arrows are tipped with the spine of the sting ray. This spine is so barbed that once it goes in, it stays in, infection begins and death results. They use this spine to tip twelve foot spears also.

These fellows are warriors from the word go and probably have made plenty of trouble for the Japanese. With a shell trumpet they can call warriors from all villages with the speed of a telephone. He loves war dances where mock battles are fought. For these dances he oils himself from head to foot. Here is the way the oil is prepared.

About four old women sit like witches around a big pot. One stirs and the other three chew dried fish heads. After masticating the fish heads, they expell the mash into the pot. The pot has shredded coconut in it and the masticated heads are stirred, pressed and kneaded. The mass is taken out and spread in the sun for a few days. The odor is so strong it is well to keep a three-mile limit. Then the oil is squeezed out and applied to the bodies of the warriors. It serves the double purpose of reflecting the sun in dazzling fashion and causing the grip of any opponent to slip hopelessly.

Everything that goes wrong in a Ponapean's life is the fault of women. All bad habits are pinned on them. A lie is "a woman's fault." Conspiracy is "a woman's whispering." Fury is " a woman's angry voice."

Still women are in demand and all marry young. Of course, grooms have nothing to do with the marriage. The girl, for all practical purposes, is married to her mother-in-law and is her virtual slave.

Anyone from Maine or Idaho will be interested to know that potatoes grow four feet long here.

News of the Briny Deep:

Advance guards of Shellbacks and Pollywogs were reported clashing on the Freddy *Funston* front last night, Adm. Jones headquarters reported. After battling furiously up and down "A" deck for an hour and a half it was discovered that Pollywog units had wriggled out and Shellbacks were wasting shells on each other. Adm. Jones reports reinforcements will arrive by sundown, October second.

Amen! until tomorrow.

Tradition Will Rule   October 1, 1944

Today at 1400 we passed within forty miles of the last of the Carolines. Kaping-amarangi or Greenwich Island is made up of thirty islets. In 1933 it had a population of 429 natives. It is still in Japanese hands.

Now we can turn our attention to the Admiralty Islands. By looking down there we notice on the map their proximity to previous hard fought battles. Names like Solomon Islands, Bougainville, Rabaul, Cape Esperance, Kula Gulf, New Britain, New Georgia, Port Moresby, Lae, Wewak and a dozen other names that are familiar to Navy, Marine, and Army men in the Pacific. A lot of American men lie under the sea and sand among these strange names. Some of our own crew lost their ships and mates in this part of the world. But their costly victories have paved the way for us to polish off the Japanese in another area.

On February 29th, 1944, amphibious forces from the Southwest Pacific Force under the command of Rear Adm. W. M. Fechteler (these forces included the First Cavalry Division, dismounted) conducted a reconnaissance in force on Los Negros in the Admiralty Islands. As the reconnaissance revealed insufficient enemy strength to warrant withdrawing our reconnaissance forces, the Island was promptly occupied. Covering forces were cruisers and destroyers under the command of Rear Adm. Barbey. This was a brilliant maneuver in the campaign in that part of the Pacific, conducted under the direction of Gen. MacArthur.

The Admiralties lie north and east of New Guinea, some 200 miles. They consist of one large, rugged, but fertile, island of Manus, in addition to about forty other small islands. The Bismarck Archipelago is about 400 miles southeastward.

The islands were once a German colony but were mandated to Australia by the League of Nations, after the World War. Their population is 14,000 and they cover a land area of 870 square miles. Like most of these islands their importance is chiefly strategic. The following products were exported: copra, sage, bananas, taro, yams, sugar cane and breadfruit while pearl and shell fisheries were developed. Chiefly they are known for copra and pearl. Interesting water spouts are known to arise around them.

Manus Island itself is fifty miles long and twelve miles wide, about twice the size of Guam. It is hilly with the center rising to 3000 feet. The rises are generally sharp and there is a conical mountain on the eastern end. Our harbor, Seeadler, is on the northeastern side.

Tomorrow is the big day. These boisterous ceremonies of "crossing the line" are so ancient, their derivation is lost. Ceremonies were practiced when ships crossed the 30th parallel and when going through the Straits of Gibraltor. No doubt these early ceremonies were plenty tough. They were supposed to try the crew to determine whether the young novices on their first cruise could endure the hardships of a life at sea. As is the custom, it was primarily a crew's "party." It is highly probable that the present-day ceremonies were passed on to the Angles, Saxons and Normans from the Vikings.

Neptune, the mythological god of the seas, was appeased by the seamen, and marks of respect were paid those of his underwater domain. Even the sailors came to doubt the existence of Neptune, nevertheless Neptunus Rex is today the majesty who rules in the ceremonies. The ceremonies of the Navy have been toned down considerably with emphasis placed on picturesqueness and embarrassment rather than physical injury. (I better knock off this until tomorrow night — but anyway that's what the book says.)

Some of you have asked me where all the material for these talks comes from. Up to tonight the bulk of it has come from the pamphlet "Guide to the Western Pacific" published by CinCPac and Cinpoa in August, 1944. An issue of National Geographic of June, 1942, and an article on the Gilberts and Marshalls by Comdr. Morrison in "Life" made up the rest. "Sailing Directions for Ships" often gives nautical statistics. Then there is always the help given by the Navigator, naval records, etc.

Amen! until tomorrow.

Trusty Shellbacks All   **October 2, 1944**

Hear Ye! Hear Ye! Hear Ye!

Know ye that all hands on the 1st day of October, 1944 at 2400, aboard the U.S.S. *Frederick Funston*, Latitude 0000, Longitude 153ºE., appeared into Our Royal Domain, and having been inspected and found worthy by My Royal Staff, were initiated into the Solemn Mysteries of the Ancient Order of the Deep. I command my subjects to honor and respect the bearer of the certificate as One of Our Trusty Shellbacks. Signed: Neptunus Rex, Ruler of the Raging Main.

All newly inducted Shellbacks, that is nearly all, want to thank Neptunus Rex and his court for the honor of the visit and acceptance into the Royal Order. The job was well done and will live long in our memories. Fortunately we have cards on board for all hands. Probably we are the only ship in the convoy to be so prepared. The Army will all have cards furnished by the American Red Cross in Balboa, Panama. The Navy will receive official Navy cards to match their Golden Dragon cards and they will also receive Navy certificates. We will treasure the cards and certificates and the distinction of being Shellbacks. But, oh boy, wait until we get hold of some scruvy Pollywogs!

Because this is voting day on board ship I think you will be interested in a historical coincidence. In November, 1898, the S.S. *Indiana*, an army transport, arrived in Honolulu on its way to the Philippines. On board was the 20th Kansas Volunteer Infantry under the command of then Colonel Frederick Funston. Kansas had a soldier's vote ballot and when election day came around voting booths were set up alongside the ship on the Honolulu dock. A rather amusing incident was the attempt of one captain to compel his whole company to vote the ticket of the Populist party. You will hear more about Freddy Funston in the Philippines in future broadcasts.

One of the Army officers has written a poem about the day's biggest event:

SHELLBACKS

'Tis time for Polliwogs to quake,
And all their earthly calm forsake;
For Davey Jones and Neptunus Rex
Have come upon the Funston's decks.

'Tis Shellbacks we're about to be,
Though many will suffer misery
Long ere they end the gruelling test
Which all must pass along with jest.

We Dragonbacks shall now become
Full members of the ocean's realm,
And brag to all, both now and later,
Of how we crossed the world's equator.

Amen! until tomorrow.

After three days in Seeadler harbor I thought you might be interested in some additional information about the place.

To correct a previous impression regarding the taking of the island it needs to be said that though the landings were made here on February 29th, fighting was still going on at Manus in April. A total of about 8,000 Japanese were on all the islands and it is estimated that possibly 100 are still at large in the interior. The landing force was all army, largely of the 1st and 2nd Cavalry, dismounted.

Since April the CBs have built up this base from nothing. There are now 30-40,000 men based here. The Japanese had made practically no efforts to build a base and the Australians had never developed the island's harbor.

Naturally it is the natives that attract the most attention. You have seen them around the harbor in their primitive outrigger canoes. These are Melanesian "fuzzy-wuzzies" of the same type found in New Guinea. If you consult the map in the forward recreation room and wardroom you can see where their cousins live. They are very primitive and backward though friendly and quite harmless. They did not like the Japanese who molested their women and homes. Any traffic with the natives is strictly forbidden but if you do get an opportunity to barter with them you will find they care nothing for soft money, even if it is a $100 bill. They will take quarters, which they call shillings, and will refuse half-dollars. Mainly they want cloth. The sails on their canoes are made of navy mattress covers. Their villages and the jungle itself are strictly off-limits. A good view of one of the villages can be had off our starboard bow.

Civil administration is in the hands of Australian officers. That is why all traffic on Victory Highway keeps to the left. Occasionally you may see some native policemen, trained in Australia, who are quite proud of their khaki shorts and visored caps.

The fleet landing is at Lorengan, where the government headquarters used to be. Near the landing is a thatched roofed museum with some examples of native handicraft and island shells on display. Also included is some captured Japanese equipment. One five inch naval gun has a steel plate with the mark of the Carnegie-Illinois Steel Company on it. In this same area is the fleet post office and a new open-air chapel with the bell of the old Lorengau German mission in the belfrey. The old mission was destroyed by naval gunfire when the Japanese used it.

Down Victory Highway is the officers club, CPO club, the old Salesia Coconut plantation and U.S. Naval Base Hospital #15. This hospital is well-equipped with 1500 beds and emergency overflow facilities.

At the present time there are over 1,000 ships in the harbor, the most there has ever been. Undoubtedly there will be still more. This was the staging area for the Palau operation and for part of the Morotai attack. Our sister ship, the *O'Hara* is at the other end of the harbor.

Amen! until later.

Target: Leyte   **October 14, 1944**

After an eyeful of that fleet in Seeadler Harbor it is not hard for us to imagine that we are a part of the largest operation (with the one exception of Normandy) in history. If we are considering only All-American invasions the operation against the Philippines will surely take the cake. Launched two months ahead of schedule it is still none too soon in coming.

Many believe it is the intent of General MacArthur and Admiral Nimitz to eventually land on the coast of China and unite with our allies who have been fighting single-handed with the Japanese since 1937, sometimes with little more than vague promises and sheer guts to keep them going. As one commentator said, "every foot that the Japanese take in China will

103

prolong the war for us a week.'' Now the China coast and air bases within 400 miles of it are being lost. This may mean taking Formosa after Luzon. So our work for the future has been cut out for us and there will be no end of tough fighting before the end is reached.

But the strategy for re-taking the Philippines is even larger than getting an obstacle removed and a stepping-stone created on the road to China. The P.I. are the "Watchdog of the Orient," so to speak. By taking them we can cut all of Japan's lines to Indo-China, Malay, Borneo and the Netherlands East Indies. The South China Sea is her funnel to tin, rubber, quinine, oil, tungsten and other rich strategic materials of this region. And whoever controls the Philippines controls the South China Sea.

When MacArthur left the Philippine Islands he vowed to return again. Some mistakenly think this was just a means of "saving face." But we now can see he realized the tremendous importance of these islands to the total strategy of defeating Japan. It is true that in our defeats in 1941 and 1942, we lost plenty of "face" in the Far East. Few Americans realize just how much prestige we lost. But if Japan could be defeated without taking the P.I. our prestige would return just the same, and I am sure General MacArthur would be the first to agree to it. But the P.I. are not Yaps or Ponapes. They must be taken at all costs.

It will be quite a surprise to most strategists, both in the States and in Japan when they hear the news on "Able" day. There are 7,083 islands in the Philippines, of which 2,441 have names. They range in size from Luzon and Mindanao, comparable in size to Kentucky and Indiana, to tiny pinpoint corals. General MacArthur has chosen neither the largest nor the smallest but one medium-sized island in the middle, the island of Leyte.

Probably most people will be buying up maps of the large southern island of Mindanao, with the second largest city, Davao, on it. But Leyte has eight strategic airfields on it from which Mindanao's supply lines can be cut and its effectiveness neutralized. Also we can control the inner Visayan Sea. On Leyte the beaches are sand and good for boat landings, the jungle is not too thick and there is a wide plain for tank operations. Probably for these reasons, the chief being the airfields, and because Leyte offers an easy stepping-stone to Luzon and Manila Bay, the decision will be a wise one. Now is a good time to get map-wise by consulting those maps posted in the forward and after recreation rooms and wardroom.

So far our preliminary thrusts against the Philippines have gone very well. Airfields on Morotai and Palau, 600 miles away, will put us in easy range with land-based bombers. Carrier-based planes have already raided Cebu, Luzon, Panay, Negros and Leyte encountering on the first two days "formidable" opposition which on the third day was non-existent. In seven carrier raids from August 30 to September 25 (four of them over the P.I.) 1,101 Japanese planes were destroyed. Halsey's fourth raid was met by only seven Japanese planes in the central Philippines and Mitscher's pilots found only twenty-nine planes on the ground to destroy. In the whole month of September we destroyed over 1,300 planes, close to the maximum monthly output of Japanese factories.

Amen! until tomorrow.

Magellan And Funston   October 15, 1944

In the five broadcasts left we will go from the general to the specific. As you know "Able" Day is Friday, the 20th, and if therefore, we start with the Philippines as a whole we will be talking about our little Blue Beach by Thursday.

The Philippines have had many names and many masters. No one can say where or when their strange, unwritten history begins but we do know that it is incredibly ancient. We know the Ming emperors of China called them the "Islands of the Luzones" and used to trade brass and cloth for pearl and precious woods. Even the Phoenician traders skirted their coastlines in quest of gold. The Portuguese, greatest of all ancient navigators, called them "The Islands of the West."

But every schoolboy knows that Magellan came in 1521 as the official "discoverer" of the Philippines. His name, the "Archipelago of St. Lazurus" did not stick. But Magellan was stuck, by poison arrows on the island of Mactan, between Cebu and Leyte. In 1543 a Spaniard named them "Islas Filipinas" after Don Felipe, crown prince of Spain. Gradually this came to be just "Philippine Islands" as Dutch, Portuguese, Javanese, Bornese, Chinese, Japanese, Spaniards, English and Americans scrambled for a foothold through the centuries.

Our war with Spain was short and sweet. Dewey (not the same as the Republican candidate for President) eliminated the Spanish fleet in Manila Bay on May 1, 1898. But this transfer of the islands from Spain did not end the strife in the Philippines. Active warfare continued for almost four years and, in some portions of Mindanao, continued for the entire period of the American occupation.

Now here is where the Freddy *Funston* joins the original Frederick Funston across forty-five years of history. Colonel Funston as head of the 20th Kansas Infantry Regiment was on hand on the outskirts of Manila when the Filipino insurgents began their independent war against the United States. In this campaign he won the Congressional Medal of Honor and was promoted to brigadier general. His one book, "Memories of Two Wars", contains stories of his fights in the hills and valleys of Luzon.

Not only will we be carrying on again in the Philippines, this time to help the Filipines drive out the invaders, but we have another unusual coincidence to go on. In command of the first Philippine campaign was General Arthur MacArthur, father of General Douglas MacArthur, now our Commander. General Funston's only son was named Arthur MacArthur Funston and he used to play with young Douglas. To top it all off, General Funston cinched the campaign by capturing the elusive chieftan of the insurgent Filipinos, Emilio Aquinaldo, thus becoming the hero overnight of millions of Americans.

In December, 1941, overwhelming Japanese forces struck the Philippines. The record of the heroic defense of Bataan and Corregidor, ending May 6, 1942, with the surrender of Lt. General Wainright, are still bright in American history.

One of the things that the Japanese aggression put an end to was the plan for Philippine independence promised for 1946.

I have been asked to explain the what and why of a paravane. A paravane is designed to cut mine cables. When lowered into the water it has a cable attached to its nose to the bow of the ship. Mines are anchored to bouys by cables below the surface. This cable on the mine is supposed to slide the mine down the cable attached to the paravane. Sawteeth on the paravane cut the cable causing the mine to rise to the surface where it can be exploded with a rifle shot. The depth of the paravane is determined by the hydrostatic valve.

Amen! until tomorrow.

Meet The Filipino: Your Ally   October 16, 1944

Fortunately when we consider the people of the Philippines we are speaking of our allies. On June 14, 1942 the late Manuel L. Quezon, President of the Philippines and symbol of Filipino Resistance, signed the declaration making them a part of the United Nations. The new President Osmena will return to his native land with General MacArthur and, as rapidly as military circumstances permit, will resume control of the liberated areas. Under their own leaders they will unite to help drive out the Japanese invaders. With President Osmena will be our old friend, Brigadier General Carlos Romulo, "the last man out of Bataan," who will act as Philippine Resident Commissioner. You will remember Romulo as the Colonel who spoke to the *Funston* men at the Lamb's Club dinner in New York City.

What is the Filipino like? The best answer to that is to get to know our three shipmates Alejandro Rosete, CK1c, Ernest

Augustin, CK3c, and Tony Mendoza, ST2c, all if them hard-working, likeable fellows. All three of these men were raised on the island of Luzon and have relatives there. Rosete last visited Leyte in 1939.

Racially, the Filipino is the result of a melting pot, just like many Americans. Chief elements are Malay, Indonesian and Indo-Australian. In the north there is an affiliation with Chinese, dating from many centuries when Koxinga, the great China pirate invaded the Philippines with 14,000 men. In the south are tribesmen of Borneo, Java, Sumatra and India and everywhere are traces of the curious little black Negritos, who were apparently there the longest.

The product of this melting pot is a sturdy jungleman, easily aroused to fanaticism and possessing a great pride of race. Religiously he is mainly a Roman Catholic, a result of Spanish influence. One-tenth of the Christians are Protestants. In Mindanao there are a half million Mohammedan Moros, who got their name from the Spaniards confusing them with the Moors of North Africa. There are also a considerable number of idol-worshiping pagans in the interior regions.

Add to all this, eighty odd tribes, eighty-seven dialects, the Spanish and American influence and you have the Filipino; all 16,000,000 of him.

General Funston paid tribute to the Filipino soldiers several times. Though poorly equipped and poor marksmen he was amazed at their courage under gunfire. Fortunately there are many Filipino soldiers, remnants of MacArthur's Scouts and Constables, who have been carrying on guerrilla warfare against the Japanese. On Leyte there are an estimated 2,600 of these troops who have been in touch with us at all times by radio and submarine. From them invaluable information has been obtained as regards to the Japanese defenses and movements.

But also on Leyte are 950,000 civilian Filipinos whose lives will be endangered in the attack. For months Uncle Sam has been keeping them informed as to the course of the war. The picture magazine "Free Philippines" and other material has

Sgt. Charles Carter Anderson, Jr. USMC

U.S.S. FREDERICK FUNSTON (APA 89), cruiser hull, 15,000 tons, length 492 feet, width beam 90 feet — commissioned April 24, 1943. Note landing craft (LCVPs) on sides.

Captain John E. Murphy, USN, first commanding officer 1943-44.

Captain Charles Carter Anderson, USN, commanding officer 1944-45.

Chaplain John D. Wolf, USNR

John D. Wolf today

NEWPORT   N. T. S. CHAPLAIN CORPS   1943
*Seated, left to right: C. S. Van Winkle, (now detached) (Pa.); J.
E. Crawley, (Ga., Fla.); B. D. Stephens, Senior Chaplain (Va.); T.
M. Conway, (N.Y.); J. Fonash, (Pa.) Standing, left to right: A. M.
Kulinski, (Wis.); J. D. Wolf, Editor "Recruit", (Ida., Ind.); R. H.
Carley, (Calif.) J. V. Loughlin, Senior Catholic Chaplain, (N. Y.);
G. P. LaBarre, (Miss., Va.); L. L. Bennett, (Ohio).*

Disembarking into LCVPs

LCVPs headed for beach

LCT and LCVPs circling in manuevers off Africa

Damaged ship in convoy after bombing

"H" Division - Hospital Pharmacist Mates

Supply Division — U.S.S. Frederick Funston

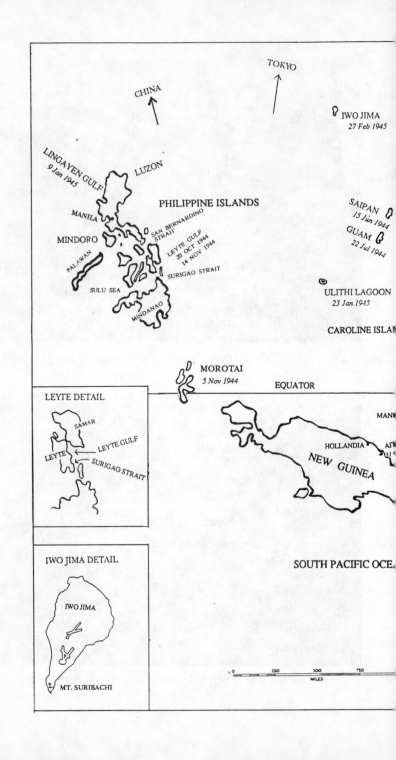

TOKYO

CHINA

IWO JIMA
27 Feb 1945

LINGAYEN GULF
9 Jan 1945

LUZON

PHILIPPINE ISLANDS

SAIPAN
15 Jun 1944

GUAM
22 Jul 1944

MANILA

SAN BERNARDINO
STRAIT

MINDORO

LEYTE GULF
20 OCT 1944
14 NOV 1944

PALAWAN

SURIGAO STRAIT

ULITHI LAGOON
23 Jan 1945

SULU SEA

MINDANAO

CAROLINE ISLAN

MOROTAI
5 Nov 1944

EQUATOR

LEYTE DETAIL

SAMAR

LEYTE GULF

LEYTE

SURIGAO STRAIT

MAN

HOLLANDIA

AIT

NEW GUINEA

IWO JIMA DETAIL

SOUTH PACIFIC OCE.

IWO JIMA

MT. SURIBACHI

0   250   500   750
MILES

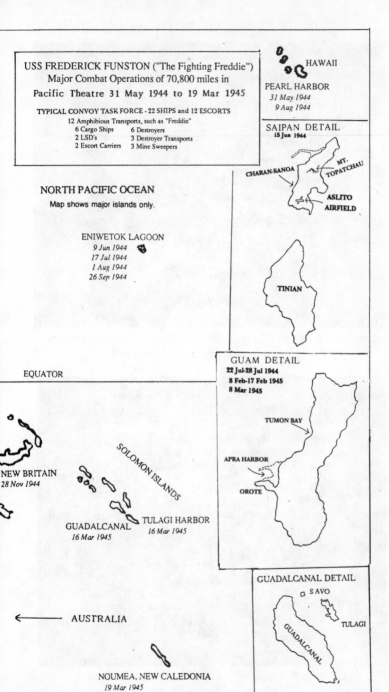

USS FREDERICK FUNSTON ("The Fighting Freddie")
Major Combat Operations of 70,800 miles in
Pacific Theatre 31 May 1944 to 19 Mar 1945

TYPICAL CONVOY TASK FORCE - 22 SHIPS and 12 ESCORTS

12 Amphibious Transports, such as "Freddie"
6 Cargo Ships   6 Destroyers
2 LSD's   3 Destroyer Transports
2 Escort Carriers   3 Mine Sweepers

HAWAII

PEARL HARBOR
31 May 1944
9 Aug 1944

SAIPAN DETAIL
15 Jun 1944

CHARAN-KANOA

MT. TOPATCHAU

ASLITO AIRFIELD

NORTH PACIFIC OCEAN

Map shows major islands only.

ENIWETOK LAGOON
9 Jun 1944
17 Jul 1944
1 Aug 1944
26 Sep 1944

TINIAN

GUAM DETAIL
22 Jul-28 Jul 1944
8 Feb-17 Feb 1945
8 Mar 1945

EQUATOR

TUMON BAY

APRA HARBOR

OROTE

SOLOMON ISLANDS

NEW BRITAIN
28 Nov 1944

GUADALCANAL
16 Mar 1945

TULAGI HARBOR
16 Mar 1945

GUADALCANAL DETAIL

SAVO

GUADALCANAL

TULAGI

AUSTRALIA

NOUMEA, NEW CALEDONIA
19 Mar 1945

Chaplain Wolf conducting services for 2nd Marine Division prior Saipan compaign, June 1944

Christmas Eve, 1944, Manus, Admiralty Islands
Chaplain Wolf — Services topside while Funston in floating drydock

TIME magazine picture of assault transports, Leyte Gulf, P.I. October, 1944 — U.S.S. Honolulu (light cruiser) in background heading for repairs after taking air torpedo. Funston in foreground. (Courtesy Press Association, Inc., and U.S. Navy)

Casualties being brought on board Funston

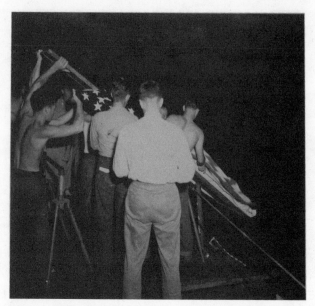

Chaplain Wolf conducting burial at sea

1945 Faculty, U.S. Navy Chaplains' School,
College William and Mary, Williamsburg, Virginia —
Chaplain Wolf, rear row, third from left

King Neptune being welcomed aboard by Captain Anderson at crossing equator initiating "pollywogs" into "shellbacks"

Funston crew observes Shellback initiation

Shellback Initiation — The Royal Barber

Shellback Initiation — The Royal Doctor, "Anesthetic?"

Shellback Initiation — Through the Garbage Tube

Shellback Initiation — Funston crossing equator
Royal doctor operates — note electric shock knife

MARINES CAPTURE IWO JIMA

Marines raise flag on Mount Suribachi, Iwo Jima, February 23, 1945. (Courtesy of U.S. Marine Corp. and from the file of the late Admiral C. C. Anderson.)

been dropped throughout the islands at the rate of over 100,000 per month. On board the Freddy is Mr. Hess of the OWI whose job is to help keep these people informed of military laws, where relief is obtainable, etc. He is also concerned with plastering the Japanese with propaganda bullets.

On the supposition that there may be some Japanese civilians on the island and that some prisoners will be taken, we have eight interpreters aboard. Four are attached to the MP's and four to Divisional Intelligence Section. If you haven't met them about the ship you will be interested to know that five are from Utah and California and three from Hawaii. Two are college graduates.

There will undoubtedly be some Filipinos working for the Japanese though it is believed that well over ninety percent of the people prefer the Americans to the Japanese. The Japanese have set up a "puppet" government in Manila headed by Jose Laurel. This government claims the Japanese gave them independence a year ago and it will call upon all loyal "puppet-men" to resist the invasion. Already they have declared war on us. In an evident attempt to win more supporters at the last moment Tokyo announced the other day that she had deposited 200,000,000 yen in a Manila bank to support Philippine independence. This sounds like a good opportunity to get some souvenir money.

Amen! until tomorrow.

A-3   **October 17, 1944**

Today is A-3 and operation King II is actually underway. Today minesweepers began a clearance sweep of the known mine barrier across the entrance to the beaches. This entrance, called Surigao Strait, is a fifteen miles channel between Homonhon Island to the north and Dinagat Island to the south.

At the same time the 6th Ranger's of General Krueger's army, supported by naval guns, will land from APD's on

Homonhon and Dinagat Islands and seize the land areas commanding the entrance. Minesweepers will proceed into the Gulf of Leyte and sweep a channel for our force.

At 1200 today the DD *Wilkes* reported a contact. Planes were sent up but no confirmation was made.

At 0030 we will be fifteen miles off Angaur, southernmost island of the Palau Islands. Few people yet realize the hard fighting that went on here and is still going on. Hardest fighting was on Peleliu where the 1st Marine Division killed 8,000 Japanese and lost 1,000 men killed and 3,700 wounded. For an island only ten miles long and five miles wide involving only one division the losses were very high, exceeding Tarawa and probably Saipan. Around the Palau's, some 400 mines were swept up which gives you an idea of how many mines the Japanese have probably sown around the good beaches of the Philippines.

We are all curious as to what the folks back home are going to read about this great invasion when they open up the morning paper Friday. On the Freddy we have Captain Pepper, Public Relations Officer attached to Divisional Headquarters and through whom correspondents send their dispatches. At Manus we also received four veteran correspondents just back from Palau. They are Stan Troutman of Acme News Pictures, Lisle Shoemaker of United Press, Don Senick of Fox Movietone and John Brennan of the Sydney Bulletin. According to these men, who believe that "the pen is mightier than the sword," the Philippine news will push the European war right off page one of every paper in the country. Radio pictures will also get back to the states as soon as news. Correspondents will be allowed to identify divisions and to give names and addresses of personalities in their dispatches. In addition the army is planning to make a full length movie of the entire invasion. On the side, I might mention that there is already a twenty-one minute film called the "Battle of the Marianas," done by Marine combat photographers and now on the market in the states.

110

Getting back to Leyte. It is the eighth largest island in the Philippines. It is about 115 miles long and only 15 miles wide at the narrowest part. A good share of it is rugged mountain but the large and fertile Leyte valley is the chief asset of the island. It is largely through its development agriculturally that the population increased from 100,000 in 1850 to well over 900,000 in 1940. The best way to describe the island's general shape would be to turn it horizontally and it will resemble a running Scotty dog trying to grab a ball, which is Biliran Island.

The chief city is Tacloban, up the forelegs. This will become American operational headquarters when it is taken. Tacloban is by air, 340 miles from Manila, 1,875 miles from Tokyo, 1,425 miles from Saipan, and about 4,500 miles from Pearl Harbor. Tonight we are on the same latitude as Davao on Mindanao and the same longitude as Osaka, Japan.

It will also interest you to know that we are now on the same time as the Philippines. It is now 1700. We are thirteen hours ahead of New York so it is 0400 there. Of further interest is the fact that the Philippines are nearly half way around the world from New York City and those of you who were with us in Italy can now say that you have been ⅔ of the way around the world thus living up to Navy posters that urged you to "Join the Navy and see the World."

Amen! until tomorrow.

A-2   **October 18, 1944**

Today is A-2 when the major portion of the Fire Support Group will enter the Gulf of Leyte and from the Transport of Fire Support Areas will cover minesweepers and reconnaissance operations of Underwater Demolition Teams, and will commence the initial bombardment of enemy positions.

Beginning yesterday a large CVE group at the entrance of the gulf will provide fighter cover for surface operations and will make fighter sweeps and bombing strikes against enemy objectives.

The bombardment ships are all old-line battleships, most of them damaged at Pearl Harbor. In fact the *West Virginia* just went back into service a few months ago. Of course this means that the new fighting ships are the ones engaged with the enemy in the northern Philippines and Formosa and out looking for the elusive Japanese fleet. The Japanese Navy is still credited with having from eleven to twenty-four battle-wagons as against our twenty-three, a number of which are still in the Atlantic fleet. Japanese carriers number ten or a dozen plus a dozen or more escort carriers but our superiority in this line entirely outclasses them. In cruisers and destroyers Japan is similarly outclassed.

The following chain of command and units are participating in this operation. Task Force 79 under Vice Admiral Kincaid is divided into the southern attack force of which we are a part, and the northern attack force. The northern force staged at Hollandia. They will land simultaneously with us in the vicinity of Tacloban and south to Palo. This force consists of the First Cavalry Division and the 24th Infantry Division.

Our southern attack force is under Vice Admiral T. S. Wilkinson and consists of the 96th Division and the 7th Division. We will land between San Jose and Dulag with the 7th Division on the left and the 96th Division on the right.

General MacArthur who is in supreme command of the entire operation will probably land from a cruiser with the northern attack force. With him will probably be President Osmena and the Philippine authorities. The actual army units involved will be under the command of Lt. General Krueger, head of the 6th Army. The 24th Corps, of which the 96th is a part, is under Major General John R. Hodge while the C.O. of the 96th is Major General Bradley.

Our attack force is protected by two carriers and their accompanying destroyers. The northern attack force which is following a more dangerous route is protected by four cruisers, seven destroyers and a couple of carriers.

Here are some further facts about Leyte. The island is definitely tropical with temperature averaging more than 80° and an annual rainfall of 100 inches. This is the wet season. From October to May is also the period of the Northeast Monsoon bringing heavy winds and rain. As you can imagine there is no such thing as a "drought."

The unit of money is the "peso", equal to about 50 cents. The peso is made up of 100 centavos. Currency for use in the islands has already been prepared and will be issued to troops. Coins of copper and silver will be flown in. Stateside currency will not be used because the enemy captured large quantities of this money when they took Manila.

In reading Funston's book the other night I discovered that when he went on the dangerous expedition into the mountains of northern Luzon, he had with him exactly eighty-nine men. Perhaps this is an omen of good fortune for us. On the other hand this library book from Honolulu, that is way overdue, has the number eighty-nine on it also.

About 1530 a destroyer sighted a floating mine. Returning to it she fired a shot, the mine failing to explode but sinking instead.

Amen! until tomorrow.

October 19, 1944

CAPTAIN'S MESSAGE TO THE CREW
PRIOR TO THE INVASION OF LEYTE.

This is the Captain.

To you officers and men of the *Funston* who man the guns, take care of the engines, run the landing boats and pilot the ship — to you and to all others connected with the success or failure of the present undertaking, *I have a message for you.* It will pay well to take heed for your very life and the lives

113

of all on board may depend upon your proper actions in the coming operation, and that your actions may be guided in the right channels, I ask of you the following.

If on the morrow — "ABLE" day — or the day after, or the days and nights that follow, you feel tired, worn out and fatigued to the point of almost quitting, *think of your fellow countrymen*, fighting with their *lives* to get across this beach-head and attain a sure foothold on the land one step closer to Japan's inner defenses. These men too are tired, much more so than you, but they *can't* give up — *and won't give up*. Their faith is in you to back them up to that point which spells Victory — *and you will not fail them*.

Most of you men have participated in the invasions of Sicily, Salerno, Saipan and Guam and did exceedingly well, too; as far as tomorrow's operation is concerned those previous invasions are like so much water over the dam. You have gained experience, it is true; however, *do not be over confident* with your successes of the past — your present operation coming up is the one that counts *now*. Go into it with all you have and keep your chins up *and your shirts on*. If you will give it your level best, if you will "deliver the bacon", so to speak, as you have previously — *and I believe you will* — yours will be not only a successful move but a strategic one as well.

The Japanese predicament summarized in a few words looks something like this — too few ships, men, machines; too much empire, — *but Japan still hopes to win!* The chief dilemma and key of Japan's worries is her increasing and continued loss of ships as she attempts to cover and protect her projected area. If she gathers the full wealth of her empire, she cannot supply her troops; then she loses the empire. If she supplies her troops, she cannot exploit the empire; then she has not enough to supply her troops and to feed her people and her machines. We, on the other hand, have advanced to a point where we are now ready to proceed from Japan's *outer empire* to her *inner empire* which includes beside Japan proper,

Formosa, Korea, Manchuria and North China — an area that Japan is trying desperately to make into one self-sufficient unit.

The Japanese may possibly oppose this operation with the major strength of the fleet. Submarine attacks on our convoys enroute to and from the objective may be expected. Enemy air reaction will probably be limited to night attacks, with possible dawn and twilight sneak raids. Hit and run attacks from hide-outs in Philippine anchorages by means of motor torpedo boats, or barges mounting torpedoes, are probable. Documents recently captured indicate that Japan now has well over 300 operational motor torpedo boats (PTs).

The straight between Homonhom Island and the northern end of Dinagat Island is mined. The straight between Homonhon and Sungi Point is mined. Mines may be present in all parts of Leyte Gulf.

Now bear this in mind, men! As we advance, the enemy's lines of defense become more consolidated and compact, and the people fighting on their homeland more determined to protect their birthright. Thus, as I said in my last talk to you, the fighting is getting tougher and tougher and you must be prepared to meet increasing enemy resistance. Do not take it for granted that you will win in a walk-over — prepare yourself for a hard, long drawn out battle — that it will entail all of this and much more, you can rest assured. That you will come out victorious is a certainty which only *you yourself* can help to bring about — by your thorough preparation for battle, your determination to conquer at all costs, and your lasting faith in the Almighty God.

C. C. Anderson
Carry On

King II Operation   October 19, 1944

We passed two mines last night. At 1800 we will be 156 miles from Leyte.

This is A-1 when minesweepers are continuing their work and underwater demolition teams are attacking any underwater obstructions developed by reconnaisance. The bombardment continues. After midnight tonight the southern attack force, beginning with the LST's will pass the entrance to the Gulf and arrive in the Transport Areas in time for H-hour, tentatively set for 1000.

The landing of our force will be made by LVT's from LST's, followed by boats from transports. The 381st Regiment, reinforced, of the 96th, will be held in reserve. Assault troops on landing will secure the slopes of Catmon Hill on the right and will push rapidly inland to secure the coastal road and the road leading to the interior from Dulag, and ultimately the airfields beyond. Opposition is expected from the veteran 16th Japanese Infantry Division and another regiment.

Air support will be available from carriers throughout the operation. Destroyers will guard the entrance to the gulf from submarines. On A plus One a large PT force will arrive.

So, we have finally arrived at the time when a momentous blow will be struck to send the enemy reeling into his corner. It is hard to realize the great significance of this operation. Major General Hodge says of it:

> *King II operation will be by far the most significant and important landing operation in the Pacific, as well as the largest initial landing yet made by U.S. Forces in any theater of this war.*

But whether the operation is big or small it will seem big to the man in it. We of the Navy will do our best to make your landings safe. The progress of outfits we have carried in the past: the 45th and 36th, now in France, the 34th in Italy, the 82nd Airborne in Germany, the 2nd Marines on Saipan and the 77th on Guam; we have followed with personal satisfaction. After six weeks with the 96th as shipmates, we will feel we have a stake in every yard of the Philippines you retake from the invader. We know you will prove yourself and we offer you Godspeed.

It is customary on the eve of battle to call on Him, without whose aid no enterprise can be ultimately successful:

Almighty God, who turnest our evil into Thy good and makest over our imperfection into Thy perfection; even as we perform the stern duties of war, free us from any base delight in destruction for its own sake.

Makes us destroyers of the works of tyranny and hate only that we may become creators of the things of peace and righteousness.

And may we so do our duty, that when the battle is over we may stand unashamed before our shipmates, our loved ones and Thee. Amen.

Amen! until tomorrow.

Hindsight   October 22, 1944

Now that the initial invasion of Leyte is history for us it would be well tonight to review the happenings of the last few days, insofar as they are available.

Since the afternoon of A-day correspondents have been beaming news back to the States and to Australia, supposedly from General MacArthur's flagship, the cruiser *Nashville*. The first news stories were much the same, telling of the amazing lack of resistance to the landings, the secure beaches and the few casualties. Then General MacArthur spoke, followed by President Osmena.

None of us had ever heard such a bombardment as was poured forth just before H-hour. It was one continuous roar. LCI's were in close, smothering the beaches with rockets and causing most of the smoke that hid the beach from our view. Planes dive-bombed and strafed the beach and made it so hot for the Japanese they were not able to make a stand until five hundred yards inland. Very few projectiles were fired at the boats though one boat from the *Bolivar* was supposedly hit.

117

Although the reception of the news in the states will undoubtedly be in keeping with the bombardment, the actual fighting seems to be light as compared with actions such as Tarawa, Saipan or Palau. On the first day the 382nd of the 96th took their objective, Catmon Hill, and planted the flag on top of it. The next day they became bogged down in an unexpected swamp. Engineers were working hard to lay a corduroy road through this swamp. On the right flank the 383rd were pushing right ahead with little opposition and seemingly not retarded by any bogs.

Today we got word that the 7th Division to our left had taken Dulag airfield, first of the eight in the valley. The northern attack force seems to have had the hardest fight on Red Beach One. But this force took the capital city of Leyte, Tacloban, a city of 5,000 people, on A-day, killing sixty-five Japanese and had six casualties. With this prize went the Tacloban airfield, in good condition. Evidently the Japanese did not dig into and defend the city as was expected. Two enemy bombers were knocked down.

About 0630 on A-day a lone twin-engine bomber came over the northern attack force, dropped some harmless bombs and was shot down. Sometime between rain squalls a lone torpedo plane laid a fish in the port bow of the *Honolulu*. This ship is supposed to have left in the company of an Australian vessel, slightly damaged also. Aside from this the only naval casualties came from a few minor hits on LST's yesterday as they were on the beach. One of them tied up alongside last evening and displayed a hole about a foot wide in her deck plate.

Last night during the smoke screen, the *Warhawk*, in attempting to get underway, collided with a battlewagon, causing little damage to either.

We have handled fifty casualties on board and now have about nineteen with us. We lost one, 2nd Lt. Perry T. Frederick of Darhart, Texas, of the Tank Battallion. It seems that several of the casualties on this operation were the result of mistaken identity or "trigger-happy" GI's. None of our ships, crew or beach party have been injured with the exception of Lt. (jg) Hicks who fell on the wet deck and broke his collar bone and Coxswain Randol who got diarrhea on the beach.

For our amazing good fortune and success there will be a General Service of Thanksgiving tomorrow afternoon on the starboard promenade deck.

Amen! until tomorrow.

From The Beach   October 23, 1944

Our course tonight is a retracing of the wake of a few days ago. It will remain this until we reach Palau and then we will head directly for Hollandia, reaching there, as the Captain said last night, on Friday the 27th.

Tonight I thought you might be interested in the story of beaches. Going ashore on H plus 22 was nothing like H-hour, so anything I relate is of personal observation at that later hour.

Unlike Saipan, there were no skeleton LVT's, LCVP's or tanks littering the beaches. There were no dead Japanese or dead soldiers to speak of. There was plenty of activity but it was all with the confidence that our superior air force was up there protecting the unloading. The only thing that fell from the skies was the ejected cases of strafing Navy planes as they peppered the front lines. All the palms except one had been blown away from the beach itself.

Moving toward the left flank of Blue One, the only notice-able enemy defenses were palm stumps used for tank traps, some barbed wire and several palm-log pill-boxes on a river's edge. Across the river we entered the beaches of the 7th Division. Here they were methodically setting up machine guns and digging trenches in case of counterattack. Among this unit we were told there was one Marine artillery unit, the only Marines in the operation.

A little ways further were the outskirts of San Jose village, a metropolis of once 5,000 souls. (Incidentally the correct population of the capital Tacloban is 31,000). Here we saw the first standing Filipino houses, called "nipas". These houses seem very flimsy by our standards. They are made of bamboo and thatch with very few nails or pieces of metal. Their present advantage is that, when easily blown down by the concussion of a bomb, they can also be easily re-built. Here were the only dead Japanese we saw, one at the side of the road and the other half-burned in a house.

We passed a Japanese cemetery that seemed to be several years old. Nearby was a white Catholic church where the natives went.

By far the greatest interest on the beach was commanded by the Filipino civilians who came from nowhere to welcome the "Americanos." They were everywhere, all ages and all sizes, trying to help us unload the boats, digging family-sized fox-holes, waving and saluting all their new friends. As a matter of fact we were not new friends but old friends for they said, "We are glad to have you back, Señors."

Some of them spoke good English, especially the young ones. They told of the low wages the Japanese paid them in forced labor, of their near-starvation in the past few months, of their mistreatment at the hands of the "superior race," and of how they were not able to buy any new clothes since the Japanese had come. Their rags bore out the latter statement. The only earthly possessions they had left were what they had on their backs, three carabaos or water buffaloes, two gamecocks and a few parakeets.

The civil affairs men who we had carried in were on the job issuing rations, water and a few tools to help construct shelters. The Freddy sent them a bundle of canvas, old blankets and water-proofing to help keep the ever-present rain out of the foxholes. Only two of the people had been injured in the bombardment.

The families were large but somehow the mother managed to keep her children clean in spite of the black sand. She had quite a time getting them all into the foxhole when she thought danger was near. But through it all there was a cheerfulness and happiness in the knowledge that the days of tyranny had ended and soon they would be back to the freedom of their homes and fields under the Stars and Stripes and the Filipino flag.

Amen! until tomorrow.

New Guinea   **October 24, 1944**

Captain Anderson is now the Commodore of the convoy.

So we are going to New Guinea! Before the war we used to think of the island as a world's-end sort of place where anthropologists study intimate facts about tolerant head-hunters. But the Japanese changed all of that. It was here that the decisive land battle has been fought that actually decided the fate of Japan in the South Pacific.

In March of 1942, MacArthur decided to hold on to Port Moresby, southeast tip of New Guinea, the last harbor north of Australia still controlled by the Allies. The Japanese needed Port Moresby as a base to launch an invasion against Australia. So they started four drives, failing in all four at the battles of the Coral Sea, Milne Bay, Buna and Sanananda, and the Owen Stanley Mountains. The Battle of the Coral Sea was the Navy's first complete victory of the war and together with Midway can be cited as the turning point in the war. At Coral Sea we lost the *Lexington*, a destroyer and tanker.

Our toehold on New Guinea wasn't secure however, until after the Battle of the Bismarck Sea when 136 Allied planes virtually wiped out a Japanese convoy that was attempting to reinforce Lae. Then came the victories of Lae, Salamaua and Finschhafen, the neutralization of the Bismarcks, the capture of the Admiraltys and Emirau.

The Hollandia attack was backed by relentless aerial surprise attacks. The Japanese had built a big base at Aitape and a bigger one at Hollandia. Three brilliantly executed attacks

121

on Hollandia destroyed or irreparably damaged all 288 planes there.

Then we made the boldest move of the Southwest Pacific War. On April 22nd, 1944, the strongest assault force ever assembled in this area, struck New Guinea at three points. The Japanese took to the hills and we seized the three big airdromes at Hollandia. This manuever had caught the Japanese flat-footed. Expecting an attack at Wewak they had transferred 3,000 Marines there and left Hollandia guarded by service troops.

From then on it was just more of the same. On the 30th of July, when we landed at Sansapor we have occupied all strategic centers in New Guinea. Then it was Morotai and then Leyte. For these later operations Hollandia has served as the headquarters of General MacArthur. The only population figures on it were general and pre-war. It says there were several hundred natives and a few white men.

New Guinea as a whole, however, is very interesting. It is a vast 1,500 mile bulwark of towering mountains, thick rain forests and terrible swamps. It has a population of 670,000 and its area is 313,000 square miles, a sixth larger than Texas. On this tropical island naked natives still live like the Stone Ages just a few miles away from modern European towns where, in pre-war days, the morning milk was delivered by airplane.

Two months from tomorrow is Christmas. The supply office has asked me to announce that there are fifty-two shopping days left. Our motto is, "Christmas is a long way off but so are you."

Amen! until tomorrow.

Slugging It Out   **October 25, 1944**

(for this section, consult glossary and maps)

The second great naval battle of the Philippines is now being fought. It began yesterday at 0750 when a large number of Tonys, Zekes, Bettys and Vals attacked the ships in Leyte Gulf. Damage was reported as minor. Interception was effective and the all-clear was sounded at 0945. Losses of the enemy are unknown. Tokyo radio said this afternoon that they had damaged two of our carriers and sunk three transports in Leyte Gulf.

At 1000 friendly submarines were ordered to the vicinity and should have reached there by nightfall. All ships were ordered to prepare for a night attack when at 0910 an enemy force estimated to be two BBs, four CAs, one CL and ten DDs reported under attack by our carrier planes in the eastern Sulu Sea. A large number of PT boats were ordered stationed in the lower Surigao strait.

Another enemy fleet consisting of four BBs, three CAs, four CLs and twelve DDs was located and engaged east of Mindoro, evidently headed for the San Bernadino Straits. The results of this battle were: two CAs and one BB damaged.

If we had any doubts about this being an all-out attack by the Imperial Navy we can forget them. A third fleet consisting of three CV's, four to six CAs and six DDs was sighted about 1500, 180 miles east of the northern point of Luzon. One CV is of Ise class. They were traveling southwest at a speed of fifteen knots.

At 1730 the main enemy fleet was reported to the north of Samar. It was estimated at six to eight BBs, fourteen CAs and eight to nine DDs. Our carrier force engaged them resulting in two CAs, one CL and one BB badly damaged. We had one CVL carrier damaged and later sunk by our own force, one heavy cruiser damaged. Our force was getting short of fighter planes what with combat losses and the loss of the carrier.

At 1620 yesterday we reported an attack on Manila harbor in which we left one Natori CL dead in the water. At 1700 one Nichi class CL and one destroyer were reported between Tortune Island and Luzon headed south at a speed of twenty knots.

Early this morning our surface forces engaged the enemy force (undoubtedly the force that was reported in the eastern Sulu Sea) at the Surigao Strait entrance to Leyte Gulf. PT boats were ready to put their sting in also, in these same waters that John Bulkley's PTs made famous a few years ago. Four enemy ships were damaged and we were closing in for the kill.

The next report said there were four BBs, eight CAs and many destroyers divided into two forces attacking our CVE force east of Homonhon Island. Evidently the force that hit Surigao Strait was larger than originally reported and though four were put out of commission a large body of them got through to their objective.

Admiral Halsley's force which was up north of Samar engaging the main enemy carrier force, immediately sent five fast carriers and four CAs to assist the CVEs and their escorts and strike at the earliest possible moment. Six fast BBs started toward Leyte and will arrive tomorrow.

To end these reports here is like finding the last chapter of a good detective story torn out. But all we can do is try and give a summary of this complicated game of chess.

Evidently the Japanese sent out three task forces all headed toward Leyte from different directions. One force from the south broke through Surigao Strait and is now engaged against the carrier force that covered the invasion. A second force was on its way down from Manila to either pass through the San Bernadino Strait or to attack our force at Leyte from the western side of the island. The main force of carriers came down from the north and engaged our main force in a hard fight, east of Luzon.

Though surface units have been engaged, this has been mainly a carrier battle. The reported box score thus far is: Japanese ships damaged or sunk: two BBs, five CAs, two CLs and four other undesignated ships. Our losses: one carrier sunk and one CA damaged.

Amen! until tomorrow.

Old as New Guinea is to the natives, it has a very short history among the western nations. Fifty-odd years ago Dutch, Germans and British were seeking to control parts of it for pioneer traders and planters. Previous to this only a few traders and missionaries had been known to visit the island that looks like a flying bird.

By 1906 the Dutch established control over the western half of the island though they had annexed this area in 1828. The Australians annexed the southeastern portion and named it the Territory of Papua. The German government took over the northeastern quarter, the Bismarck Islands and the Admiraltys and called them Kaiser-Wilhelms-Land.

Since this time the coastline has been developed into coconut plantations but the interior was left to the explorers, goldminers and a few more venturesome missionaries. During the World War an Australian naval force took over the German Kaiser-Wilhelms-Land and since that time the eastern half of New Guinea has been British and the western half Dutch. Several years ago this second largest island in the world broke into the news again when Amelia Earhart took off from there to Howland Island when she was inexplicably lost.

Be that as it may, the island was discovered by pygmies milleniums ago. These are the same Negritos who we mentioned as the original inhabitants of the Philippines. Some of them went on to Australia. These people had a wood-shell-fiber inventory of pre-Stone Age tools and weapons. Later they mixed with the Polynesians and Melanesians until now they are, in general, much like the natives we saw at Manus.

The natives are called Papuans. They are tall and black and generally wear their hair all fluffed out in a large mop. Their houses are almost always built on piles, sometimes unusually high and long. Sometimes they even have large communal houses divided up like an apartment house.

Like the natives at Manus they spent a great deal of time in dugout canoes. To make a large boat they simply tie several dugouts together, put a deck over them and rig large sails. They are fond of music from flutes and drums.

Instead of asking for a shilling, these natives are liable to put the bee on for a guilder or florin, worth, as far as I can find out, about sixty-eight cents. Because their numerals only go up to five, they can only count in series of five. Cannibalism was formerly widespread here and is still practiced in out of the way regions. To be brutally frank fellows, we are in one of the most primitive areas left on the face of the globe. With the remnants of the Japanese 18th Army still in the interior struggling for survival, it is still more primitive.

Amen, until the next trip!

American Wooden Shoes   October 28, 1944

Here is your on-the-spot report of Hollandia or perhaps I should say Dutch New Guinea. Hollandia itself is nothing but where the government buildings and supply depots were. Now it is pretty hard to find a Dutchman. On the township site is the fleet P.O., some docks and many buildings being erected night and day. Some of the men didn't even know where Hollandia actually was.

But foreign influence is there just the same. As at Manus, everyone drives on the left-hand side. Soldiers are paid in Guilders, exchange value fifty-three cents. The Guilder note has a lot of Dutch writing on it and a picture of Queen Wilhelmina; but they were printed in the USA.

Manus was mainly a naval supply base. Hollandia is mostly Army. Installations on the beaches of the bay are not as numerous as those back in the hills. After traveling around half the bay we therefore headed inland. The hitch-hiking method served the purpose. The roads have all been laid by the CBs and Army Engineers in the past six months. It is rather marvelous what they have done in this time. Since most of the land is red and white clay, the roads are packed with this substance, and though smooth, are slippery when wet.

MPs were stationed at intervals and patrolled this busy highway in white jeeps. The road winds up and in and around the hills. Several wrecked vehicles at the bottom of some told us why all the fuss.

From high up we could view some of the native thatched villages built out over the water on stilts. One enemy merchant ship was sunk in a small bay. We passed native laborers many times. They are doing a great deal of work for us. Like the Filipinos they seemed to like the Americans, always waving and smiling and bumming smokes. Most were dressed in a kind of uniform of khaki shorts, and GI machetes, though a few still wore colorful lava-lavas (lap-laps).

To the side of this highway were encamped thousands of GIs. They lived in elevated tents with wooden floors and seemed in high spirits. Probably they were thinking of how lucky they are compared with their buddies in the deserts of Saipan, Palau and Leyte. Also along this road was a small cemetery and an 8,000 bed hospital, to which our casualties were taken.

Twenty miles inland we reached the fresh water Lake Sentani where good swimming is to be had. It could have been any of the beautiful mountain lakes at home. Thirty miles inland we came to the airfields. High above them on a commanding hill was General MacArthur's former headquarters. Naturally we went up to pay the respects of Freddy Funston but the general was not home.

It is impossible to adequately describe the beautiful view from this altitude. Below were many mountain lakes surrounded by thick jungle vegetation and occasional patches of meadow. Above us was a much higher mountain with steamy clouds laying a mantle over the top.

Let's see now, I told you about the scenery, natives, GIs — Oh yes, I almost forgot. There are several hundred lovely WACS and Army nurses here. They were very attractive in the latest fashions of khaki slacks, shirts, coveralls and fatigue hats. But they all remembered to use cosmetics. Come to think of it maybe that's why the men were in such good spirits.

The *Funston* family welcomes a baby girl each to Lt. (jg) and Mrs. Sol Weiner and Lt. (jg) and Mrs. Wm. Downey. Are there more?

Amen! until tomorrow.

Aitape, Rimes With Unhappy   November 1, 1944

Tomorrow we shove off for Morotai, still in the Nether-lands East Indies and about half way to the Philippines. At Aitape we embarked the 112th Cavalry combat team, under command of Brigadier General Cunningham, who is also aboard. Since we only have about 1,000 troops aboard it is possible that we will pick up more at Morotai.

Over at Aitape, landings were made the same time as they were made at Hollandia. April 22nd. Fighting did not stop until July. By those landings we gained control of the Tadji airstrip.

Although Aitape was secured, fighting has continued in the vicinity of Wewak, forty miles further east. An estimated 8,000 Japanese troops are still holding out. Starvation has so effected the troops that they are described weighing as low as forty-three pounds and eating their own dead.

Throughout British New Guinea there is now a general ex-odus of American troops and airforce, being replaced entirely by the "Aussies". Strategy seems to demand that we move north through the Philippines to the China coast. The British meanwhile will have the task of cleaning out the isolated East Indies; Java, Sumatra, Celebes, Borneo.

Last night was Hallowe'en with reportedly only Lt.(jg) Com-tess and Ens. Meyer being scared, having been left at Hollan-dia. Shipmates extend their sympathy to W. R. Cooper, StM, who lost his mother, B. T. Prosser, Slc, and J. A. Pimental,

MM2c, who lost their fathers and to L. H. King, BM2c, who lost his brother at Peleliu.

Amen! until tomorrow.

The Horseless Cavalry   November 2, 1944

The 112th Cavalry is a former National Guard outfit from Texas. Possibly fifty percent of them are now "foreigners", replacements from outside the lone star state. Some of them have been away from the states thirty months and many of them for two years. The outfit is credited with three engagements; Woodlark Island in the Solomons; Arawe, New Britain, and Driniumoor River, British New Guinea, which is near Aitape. Since many of the *Funston* men have been on five invasions you fellows can get together and swap lies with each other.

You don't have to have a very long memory to recall when MacArthur landed on Morotai. Three months to the day after Saipan and on the same day Marines invaded the Palau Islands, September 15th it was, just six weeks ago.

Here MacArthur's Sixth Army troops swarmed ashore under cover of heavy air and sea bombardment. As at Tarawa, troops had to leave their landing boats at a reef, wade through waist deep water before they hit the beach. There were no Japanese to be seen. Only U.S. casualty: an officer who broke his leg.

At Morotai, engineers started building an airfield immediately. Since then bombers have been used to cover the Philippines, 300 miles away. These fields will also find use against the Netherlands East Indies at some future date.

Amen! until tomorrow.

Today about 1300 the Freddy crossed the equator for the fourth time. Old Neptune blew a heavy gust of wind on us as we again cross his domain's boundary.

If you have been looking over the maps lately to find all these new and strange places like Morotai, you may have noticed how the Netherlands East Indies seems to form stepping stones between Australia and Asia. During the Ice Age, when so large a part of the waters of the world were tied up in the Polar ice caps, the level of the oceans was greatly lower than it is now. At that time, so geologists believe, the western islands of this region were connected with the continent of Asia, while the eastern part was a part of a much larger Australia.

This theory is further strengthened by the fact that the waters between the Malay Peninsula, Sumatra, Java and Borneo nowhere are over 100 fathoms. The sea between New Guinea and Australia is also very shallow.

The relative size of these Indies can best be seen if we lay a map of the States over it. Taking where we are at this moment as Cape Hatteras, Virginia, the westernmost part of the Indies (Sumatra) would extend to the west coast. Morotai would be up in Lake Erie.

This is the largest archipelago in the world, 4,000 miles west to east and 1,200 miles north to south. In this area are very rich deposits of rubber, quinine, tobacco, sugar and tea that will now be cut off from Japan by our growing control of the air and supremacy of the sea.

Most of our acquaintance with the area has been from such books and movies as "The Story of Dr. Wassel". However, at least one important naval battle took place here, the Battle of the Java Sea in 1942. At this time the enemy sank or captured most of the Allied ships in the area. The *Houston* and *Perth* were lost in this action, the *Marblehead* damaged.

From time to time we can answer any questions you have during this evening broadcast. Just leave them in the ship's chaplain's office on "A" deck. Tonight someone asked what is the "G.I. Bill of Rights".

The G.I. Bill of Rights provides that any man who was in active service on or after 16 September 1940 and before the end of the war, and who possesses an honorable discharge, is eligible for a refresher or retaining course not to exceed one year at an approved educational institution of his own choice.

"In addition if you were not twenty-five years of age at the time of entering service, and you complete one-year satisfactorily, you may continue in school up to four years, depending on your length of service. If you were over twenty-five when you entered service you must give evidence that your education was disrupted.

"While in school a student can select his own courses. He will be given a subsistence allowance of fifty dollars per month if he has no dependents and seventy-five dollars if he has. Furthermore, the government will pay the cost of tuition, laboratory, library and health or similar fees and books, supplies and other equipment. No payments for any one person shall exceed $500."

Amen! until tomorrow.

We Step In Where Captain Cook Feared To Tread   November 4, 1944

Tomorrow about 0700 we will arrive off the southeast coast of Morotai. Presumably we will be there for five days and though it is generally thought we will go to the Philippines, there are no definite orders to that effect as yet.

Morotai is kind of a suburb of Halmahera. With several adjacent islands they make up the Molucca Islands. At one time this group was so full of pirates who controlled the Molucca Straits, that Captain Cook himself chose to sail around them at safe distance when traveling from Australia to China.

131

Halmahera is the largest of the group. It has a shape very similar to the Celebes, an octupus with five long tentacles. The Japanese probably expected us to attack Halmahera but MacArthur pulled another one of his unexpected strategies when he landed on adjacent Morotai instead.

A strait of only 10½ miles separates Morotai from Halmahera so we may be able to see the latter on our port side in the distance. Morotai itself is forty miles long. The Sabatai range of mountains sometimes reaches as high as 4,100 feet in height down its center.

Around the river banks are forests of sago trees and in the interior are dammar forests. The villagers on the coast collect dammar gum for export, which is used to form a colorless varnish. There are plenty of fish in the adjacent waters. These constitute one of the main items of the staple diet.

Last night we dealt with the educational features of the G.I. Bill of Rights. However, a lot of the fellows will not want to continue their education but will want to find a job right away. What about them? The government does not promise every returning vet a job. However, a Veteran's Placement Service Board has been set up which will seek to find work for the veteran for which they are best fitted. It will act as a clearing house for jobs and men and also try to persuade employers to give veterans priorities for jobs.

If a man is unemployed until he gets the job he is suited for, the government will give him an allowance up to $20 per week. But he may not refuse a job for which he is fitted or quit without good reason. The benefit is limited to a year.

The fellow who wants "to be his own boss" will find help too. He may borrow to buy and equip his own business place and have $2,000, or not more than half, of his loan guaranteed.

Supposing you want to buy a home. What then? Again the government will guarantee half of a veteran's loan up to $2,000. So he has the assurance of a fifty percent guarantee on a $4,000 loan to buy or build a house or farm. Interest is limited to four percent and the government pays the first year's interest on the part guaranteed. The government will also make sure the veteran is not getting "gypped" by speculators and that he will have a chance to pay off his obligation.

The last provision in the bill has to do with health. Many men are going to need medical, dental or hospital treatment before they can get back to normal civilian lives. The government has already begun to spend a half billion dollars for new hospitals to supplement the ninety-four veteran hospitals already established.

If a man needs an artificial arm, leg, teeth, etc. they will be provided with these together with the training in their use. All this is without any cost whatsoever. These hospitals will always be open to service men regardless of whether his illness or injury was suffered in the service. So there you have the "G.I. Bill of Rights."

Amen! until tomorrow.

Betty Drops In   November 6, 1944

Now here is the corrected story of what happened last night. About 0130 radar picked up twelve enemy planes headed this way. Six of these planes got through and dropped about six bombs in the vicinity of the airstrips on Morotai in three different raids.

The bombs were of the heavy, new type, designed to explode several hundred feet off the ground, throwing an incendiary phosphorus over a wide area. As far as we can learn no one was killed.

The Japanese planes were identified as two-motor Bettys, probably from bases in Celebes or Borneo. Two of them were shot down, one by a black widow night fighter and the other by ack-ack.

The same type of attack has been held here nightly for the past few weeks with one exception. Sometimes the attacks are stronger than at other times. It is no wonder that they pick on the airstrips. It is hard to imagine just how big they are without actually seeing them.

If you were amazed at Manus' or Hollandia's mushroom growth, you would be bowled over at what has been done here in just seven weeks. With nothing to start with and no native labor to help, the CBs and engineers have done another one of these jobs that would make Henry Kaiser's shipbuilders turn green with envy. Miles of roads, bivouac areas and airstrips are the result.

Amen! until tomorrow.

Farewell With No Regrets   November 10, 1944

Upon leaving the night life of Morotai behind us, few of us felt like shedding any tears of regret. In five days and nights we had eleven general quarters, the total loss of sleep amounting to eight hours, thirty-nine minutes.

After the first night's experience the rest of the raids were somewhat of a letdown. This feeling to be shared by those ashore, who regarded this as an unusual raid. The reason for this was that the enemy had seldom done any actual damage to our planes. Like our gunners, the AA men were still fretting over not bringing down those Bettys when they were so well spotted in the beam of radar-controlled searchlights.

Our convoy remains the same as before. We have the addition of 300 personnel aboard attached to the ground forces of the 7th AAF. Our cargo was changed considerably because we will have only eight hours to unload the ship at Leyte.

Final election returns back home are expected to show a record vote of about fifty million. In the crew of the *Funston*, there are 363 eligible voters. Of this number ninety voted by state ballot, sixteen by federal ballot making a total of 106 votes cast, or a percentage of twenty-nine of the eligible personnel.

We were asked why we didn't change our time since we crossed a time zone between New Guinea and Morotai. This was true, but New Guinea, Morotai and the Philippines are now all on the same time. Some while ago you set your watches back an extra hour and had forgotten about it. Therefore the adjustment has already been made and our time will not change.

Tomorrow night we will begin a series of talks on the Philippines. Tonight here are some odds and ends of news from around the ship:

1. In the "March of Time" at Wednesday night's movie, CPhM Carney was recognized as one of the men in the shots of Guam, where he once had duty. He was drinking milk at the bar in the Navy ship's service.

2. In Hollandia, a group of officers saw an animal right out of a zoo. It had a long tail and strong paws with the appearance of a monkey. But its fur was white with brownish-red splotches over it. To satisfy Lt. Sand, the native carrying it told him it was a "coosy-coosy".

3. Our candidate for the most optimistic man on the ship is Lewis Walker, SK who had his wife buy two tickets to the Rose Bowl game.

4. A letter from our shipmate A. R. DePasquale, wounded at Guam, tells us the shrapnel was removed from his eye and he is now undergoing treatment in a hospital near his home town.

5. Our former quartermaster Lagotic, is reported to be a full Lt. and skipper of an LST.

Amen! until tomorrow.

The Nape Of The Neck   November 12, 1944

The fighting around the town of Ormoc is still going on. At one time we described the shape of Leyte as that of a scotty dog running after a ball. Of course the dog is in a vertical position with the belly toward us. With this in mind you can picture Ormoc Bay as the space between the ear and the nape of the neck. The town of Ormoc itself has a population of several thousand and is situated at the end of the bay. It is heard that the enemy has landed reinforcements from Cebu, which is only twenty-five miles away and Mindanao which is twelve miles at the nearest point to Leyte. Since our objective is to reach Luzon and then China as soon as possible, this move of the enemy would seem to be something of a delayed action plan. We don't mind killing them on Leyte but time is a precious commodity out here right now.

The nearness of these islands to each other makes us realize that the Philippines themselves are 7,000 separate islands, most of them very small. Less then half of these have names. The largest, of course, are Luzon on the northern end and Mindanao on the southern extremity.

All these islands together have an area only a little smaller than the British Isles. They occupy a similar position off the coast of Asia as England and Ireland off the coast of Europe. That is why they are strategically so important. From the Philippines we can control vital areas of Japan, China, Burma, Indo China and the Netherlands East Indies. It is roughly 700 miles from the closest Chinese position near Canton, sixty-five miles from the big Japanese fortress of Formosa, only 500 miles from Palau and 500 miles from Indo-China. In addition they are 4,900 miles from Pearl Harbor and 2,000 miles from Darwin, Australia.

Amen! until tomorrow.

To His Ancestors   **November 13, 1944**

This morning's general quarters was caused by enemy planes in the vicinity. They numbered anywhere from six to ten, one of them actually in sight of escorts off our starboard bow. Later, friendly planes were reported between us and the enemy planes.

Who could describe the mixture of emotions that ran through us this afternoon as that Japanese torpedo-plane threatened the ships of our convoy? We were first aware of her presence by the rapid five-inch fire of the DDs on our starboard side. Then the "Jill" broke out of a cloud and began to dive parallel to the convoy. We were in a series of emergency turns as she banked over the last row of ships and came on through the ack-ack thrown up to meet her, strafing as she came in. Over the second row she dropped her fish. But she was too high and the torpedo skipped away harmlessly. Foolishly she began to rise and bank. When she did this she was hit square by a five-inch burst from an LSV and dropped like a plumb line into a watery grave. It was a dramatic and thrilling moment for all topside, mixed with fear that she would strike her mark. The relief was evident as a tremendous cheer went up at the kill.

All this makes us acutely conscious of the fact that we are in a combat zone again. Tonight at midnight we enter Leyte Gulf passing between the islands of Dinagat on the port side and Homonhon on the starboard side. From there it is sixty-seven miles to our beach. We will arrive off our designated beach, just to the north of our former beach and at the mouth of the San Pedro Bay, about sunrise. Unloading should begin immediately and, if all goes well, we should finish and be out of there by sunset. All hands are cautioned about working around open hatches and holds. We have had two casualties lately due to carelessness in these vicinities.

Tomorrow you will have a chance to meet the Filipino. You will find him very friendly and courteous to you. There was no foolin' in the joy of the natives at our coming on October 20th. They had been waiting for us for a long while and knew we would return. The friendship of these people was made long ago, when they discovered we were not just another foreign power trying to muscle in — we wanted a partnership leading to self-government and they have responded in gratitude with their goodwill and blood.

You will find the Filipino generous and hospitable, unselfish and happy. He believes the U.S. is the greatest country in the world and General MacArthur is his No. 1 hero. And he thinks that you, as an American soldier, are a representative of the finest people in the world.

Since this is the last broadcast with the 112th Cavalry and 5th AAF aboard we take this opportunity to wish you good luck and Godspeed. We have seen a lot of outfits but you have left a fine impression with us that equals any others. We have every confidence that you will acquit yourselves as well as you have in New Guinea.

Amen! until tomorrow.

Tare, Victor, George   November 15, 1944

Yesterday we were the first ship unloaded. The Commodore gave us a "very well done" for this feat. All hands, especially the TQM, Lt. Tench, and the officers and men who manned the hatches, should feel justly proud of their work. All due credit should go to the hard-working soldiers in the holds. The 112th was an all right outfit.

U.S.S. *Catskill* was given credit for the plane shot down 13 November.

A few details have come to us regarding the sinking of the carrier *Princeton*. A shore-based divebomber hit the *Princeton* at 2,000 feet. Smashing through the hangar deck, a 1,000-pounder exploded on the third deck and blew up the magazine. Thirty minutes later the order to "abandon ship" was given and nine hours later American guns and torpedoes sent her to the bottom.

But the most heroic action of the Philippines naval battle took place between the Japanese force of four BBs, seven CAs and twelve DDs that broke through the San Bernadino Straits and attacked a force of baby carriers off the eastern coast of Samar.

To cover the retreat of the vulnerable baby tops, one DE and two DDs, representing all the resistance that could be summoned at the moment, straddled the path of the on-coming Japanese fleet. One DD laid a smokescreen, then darted into it to deliver a torpedo attack at close range. The other two followed it up.

In the breather provided, the baby tops, blessed with a southeast wind, had time to launch their planes. More planes of the 3rd fleet came up. Under that force they sunk one CA, and one DD; damaged three BBs or cruisers and a DD. It was in this battle that we lost two CVEs, two DDs and one DE with "considerable casualties".

Here are a few announcements:

A variety of Christmas cards have been designed by Dr. Lemon and Nix, QM2c, and will be available as soon as we can get hold of some V-Mail to mimeograph them on.

Payday is coming up and these special Pearl Harbor Day warbonds are on sale for Christmas at the Supply Office in return for cold cash.

English classes in grammar and spelling will be held each day at 1315 in the library until we reach Manus.

These broadcasts of Guam and Leyte campaigns will be mimeographed soon and available for distribution.

Amen, until the next trip.

Lingayen Gulf, Luzon, P.I.

A compilation of broadcasts to ship's personnel and troops on board U.S.S. Frederick Funston (APA-89)

As you may already know, we are headed for New Britain, not Great Britain as we were this time last year, but New Britain. Specifically we should arrive in Borgen Bay on the northwestern coast tomorrow noon. Here we expect to pick up troops.

To reach New Britain we skirt the eastern coast of the Admiralties and then cross the Bismarck Sea. New Britain lies off the western coast of New Guinea, a part of what is called the Bismarck Archipelago, made up of New Britain, New Ireland and New Hanover besides some lesser islands. New Britain is second only to New Guinea in this group and is as big as Massachusetts, Rhode Island and Connecticut combined.

The island is a rough crescent with the concave side to the north and with the western tip somewhat farther south than the eastern. It is about 330 miles long and 56 miles wide. The coasts have plenty of coral around them. There are some good-sized mountains and several active volcanoes. On our end is "The Father" with two "Daughters" nearby. In 1937 The Mother erupted and threatened the destruction of Rabaul, which was evacuated.

Like the Admiralties and Northeastern New Guinea, these islands are now under Australian mandate since World War I. The capital was at Rabaul until September 1941 when it was moved to Lae, New Guinea. The people are the Melanesians that have been familiar sights to us lately.

Rabaul is the largest town. It was well-laid out and attractively planned by the Germans in 1910. It is in this area that most of the cultivated acres of coconuts are found. Around the coast are some eighteen to twenty villages.

The vegetation is luxuriant and heavy where nearly any fruit or vegetable will grow. Coconuts and cocoa are exported.

We have heard more about Rabaul than anywhere else in New Britain. Arawe, where the 112th Cavalry fought, is on the south coast. Rabaul, however, with its excellent, sheltered harbor was the key position of the Japanese control of the

143

Solomons, and islands to the south. In November-December 1942, Rabaul was repeatedly attacked by our carrier planes and land-based planes from the Solomons. Japanese men-of-war were damaged or destroyed. The base is still in enemy hands but has been neutralized.

Lt. Treble says an officer aboard the *Monrovia* heard a Tokyo broadcast which listed ships the Japanese had sunk. Among them was the *Funston*. We should be flattered to be so honored by both Berlin and Tokyo.

Amen! until tomorrow.

The Sunshine Boys   **December 10, 1944**

We should arrive for the third time in Manus, tomorrow morning. This week we have a possible "dry run" ahead of us.

Our new shipmates are men of the 3rd Battallion, 108th Regiment, 40th Division, under the command of Major Thrall, and a portion of the 7th Evacuation Hospital under Colonel Lobban. Altogether they total about 1,200 officers and men, so we will be travelling light this trip.

The 40th Division went overseas in the last war as replacements. Some years ago they were formed into National Guard units. Originally from California, Nevada and Utah, the outfit was called out to defend the south California coast after Pearl Harbor. Scheduled to go to the Philippines, Alaska and then Ireland, they were finally sent to defend the outer islands of the Hawaiian Islands.

After intensive training in Hawaii the 40th went to Guadalcanal to stage for Kavieng in New Ireland. While on loaded transports this operation was called off, quite a let-down, as you can imagine. Kavieng and Rabaul were by-passed, as you know.

Then the division was sent to New Britain to relieve the 1st Marine Division at Gloucester and Borgen Bay and the

112th Calvary at Arawe. One regiment had some mopping up to do in this sector.

Only about ⅓ of the original 40th remains since they came overseas. Some of the men have been out thirty-four months. They know as much about living in the jungles as could be known. So far no one else has complained of leaving the dust and mud of New Britain behind.

This will be the first combat operation for the division. Three years pent-up energy is bound to make it rather tough for the Japanese that get into their way. But after so many disappointments, some will be skeptical until the first bomb drops or first bullet whistles. We'll try not to disappoint you again, fellows.

The insignia of the division is a sun with twelve rays on a blue diamond. Probably because of their atabrine complexion they are called the "sunshine boys."

If you men will recall your Schofield barracks' days, you will remember having met Frederick Funston before. The gate and street of that same name is in remembrance of the same great general. Later I will tell you more of his exploits in the same area where you will be doing battle. If you want to know more about our ship, just give a sailor a chance. We have been in five invasions and the crew isn't a bit bashful about telling you of them. Keep your fingers crossed when he starts going into details however. Chances are he has a good imagination. We have a fine ship and a clean ship and we hope that while you enjoy your vacation aboard, that you will help keep her that way.

The crew will be interested to know that inquiries have been made about the picture of the "Freddy" in the November 6 issue of *Time*. As soon as we find out where we can get copies, you will be informed.

Amen! until tomorrow.

Lae And Salamana   **December 16, 1944**

We are on our way to make a "dry run" in Huon Gulf in eastern New Guinea. We will reach there Monday morning.

The practice will last about two days after which we will return to Manus. We will be in Manus for Christmas. Then we can begin thinking of a good way to start 1945.

To reach Huon Gulf we skirted the eastern end of the Admiralties, crossed the Bismarck Sea and will go through the Vitiaz Strait between New Britain and New Guinea. Because we have two days to make the distance of 555 miles, it is likely that part of tomorrow we will circle outside of Huon Gulf.

Our practice beaches lie between the towns of Lae and Salamaua, names already familiar in the annals of this war. The Japanese landed here early in 1942 and built up bases for future operations against Port Moresby and the remainder of the peninsula still in Allied hands. On March 10, 1942, we sent our first big air raid over these two bases.

On the night of June 29-30, 1943, Allied troops made a successful landing on Nassau Bay, about ten miles south of the Japanese base at Salamaua and began to move up toward the big base. Navy PT boats harassed enemy landing barges and prevented reinforcements from landing.

On September 3rd our amphibious forces were ready to move against the enemy's naval and air bases in Huon Gulf area. The Australian 9th Division landed near Nopoi. Air attacks were heavy. During the following days other task forces escorted more landing craft to the beaches, successfully fighting air attacks and on September 7-8, bombarded positions in the vicinity of Lae. On September 11th, Allied forces captured Salamaua and five days later took Lae.

The next objective was Finschhafen on the eastern end of the Huon Peninsula. On the morning of September 22, a task force of destroyers and landing craft landed a strong Australian force. On October 2nd Finschhafen was captured and PT boats sank a number of enemy barges loaded with troops attempting to get clear of the island. The DD *Henley* was lost in this action.

On February 13th, a final occupation of the Huon Peninsula was completed by the meeting of the Australian units with the U.S. 32nd Division, now in Leyte.

No mention of the taking of Lae and Salamaua is complete without the Battle of the Bismarck Sea. On March 1st a big enemy convoy was sighted off Ubili Island bearing reinforcements to the Japanese garrison at Lae. A total of 136 land-based planes, practically all we had, attacked the convoy for three days running. The Japanese lost three cruisers, seven DD's, twelve merchant ships, 15,000 troops and about 90,000 tons of shipping. This battle is recognized as an invasion classic for the Mitchells developed masthead bombing to a science here.

Amen! until tomorrow.

Another Step
In The Philippines   December 17, 1944

Today we passed through strategic Vitiaz Strait between New Guinea and New Britain. The beauty of the Huon Peninsula on our Starboard side belied the heavy fighting that went on here just a year ago. When in the vicinity of Finschhafen we turned eastward to make a wide circle before reaching our anchorage tomorrow morning.

Tonight we are just off the southwestern coast of New Britain. Here on the port side will be Salamaua Peninsula with the port of the same name on a narrow strip joining the mainland. Around this area are dense woods and in the western background are the Kuper and Herzog ranges of mountains.

Before the war Salamaua was a gold miners' town. Here was a hotel, two stores, the administrative headquarters of the district, a government hospital and an airfield. Miners flew everything from heavy machinery to race horses from here over to the Morobe gold fields in Wau. Some out-of-the-way miners had their morning milk delivered by plane.

Separating Salamaua and Lae is eighteen miles and the Markham River. You can pick out Lae by a big hill with a groove in it and a stately tree growing in that groove. Since

1941 Lae has been the capital of all mandated New Guinea. Here was a government agriculture station and another airfield. Neither Lae nor Salamaua probably resemble very much their pre-war appearance.

The taking of Mindoro Friday was expected by most of us. The amphibious operation was probably launched from Leyte Gulf in LST's, LSM's and LCI's. The route probably lay through Surigao Strait and around through the Sulu Sea.

Fortunately, the Mindoro operation came cheaply. By it we cut the Philippines in two and gained possession of at least two airstrips which can be widened and improved for fighter planes.

The island itself is about as rugged and undeveloped as Samar. It lies no more than fifty-five miles south of the entrance to Manila Bay and its northern coast is only a twelve mile step from Luzon. Mindoro is the seventh largest island in the Philippines. It is high and mountainous with narrow coastal lowlands on the eastern coast. Health conditions, especially malaria, are not good. This probably accounts for the imperfect development of the interior and the small population. Calapan, overlooking Verde Passage, is the capital.

Amen! until tomorrow.

December 29, 1944

TO: All officers and men of 40th Infantry Division Reinforced.

This Christmas is particularly significant to members of this Task Force in that it finds us poised and ready to assist in the destruction of Japanese military forces. The day of actual combat is near at hand.

I have the utmost confidence that each and every member of my command will do his part to bring about a speedy and successful termination of this conflict and thereby contribute to returning "Peace on earth good will toward men."

With deep appreciation for the loyalty and cooperation you have shown since my assumption of command, I extend to you Christmas Greetings and my best wishes for a successful and victorious New Year.

Rapp Brush
Major General, USA

Target: Luzon   December 31, 1944

Tonight finds us finally on the last lap of another big operation. At the moment we are on our usual route to Leyte Gulf, via the Palau Islands. We do not stop at either one but continue to our target which is, as you know from the army maps about ship, Lingayen Gulf, on the western side of Luzon. Our route will be treacherous and will mean many sleepless nights for us. But we will discuss that later.

Our convoy numbers twenty ships and five escorts. Several carriers are nearby. The *Rocky Mount* is our flagship with Rear Admiral Royal in command. Our speed is twelve knots. We will cross the equator for the 6th time at 2400.

Tomorrow is New Year's day and brings back memories to the men of the Freddy of a year ago when on New Year's eve we anchored in Gravesend Bay, L.I., after seven months in the Mediterranean. It meant ten days leave and liberty in New York City, but that is only a fond memory tonight.

Christmas is not so far behind us however, so here is a little doggeral written by one of the ship's officers:

Christmas time brings this lament,
I wish't I wuz where you has went,
Or you wuz here where I is at,
Or something similar to that.

'Cause when I is whereat you ain't,
I'ze bound to make a big complaint,
And even Christmas ain't so hot,
When I is at where you is not.

While we were in Manus, three of our crew were commended by the commander of an LCI for their efficient and cooperative work. They are Coxwains Watkins and Jedach and MoMM3c, Kolisko. Congratulations!

That long awaited turkey and ice cream is on the menu for tomorrow according to Commissary Officer Therien.

All men who wish to enter a ship's chess tournament will sign up in the library before noon tomorrow. Captain Shulig of the Army is in charge. The tournament is open to Army and Navy, officers and men.

Amen! until tomorrow.

Hindsight:
Tarawa — Foresight: Manila   January 1, 1945

Happy New Year Shipmates!

Looking back over 1944 we can see a great deal of progress in the war. When the year started we had just secured Tarawa and Makin in the Gilberts; Russia was fighting along the Dnieper River; and the allies were sloshing through mud toward Rome.

Then in January and February we took Kwajalein and Eniwetok atolls. The Marshalls were secured. Air attacks were begun on Truk and the Marianas that same month. Then MacArthur acted, by-passing Rabaul and Kavieng, he landed on Los Negros February 29th and later on Manus. In April he jumped to Aitape and Hollandia. Wakde and Biak followed.

In Italy the landings on the Anzio beachhead finally led to the fall of Rome in June. The long-awaited invasion came off in June also and within the next six months the Allies crossed the German borders. The Russians moved swiftly through Romania and Bulgaria in the spring and were well on the road to Vienna at the year's close.

In March the "Freddy" sailed into Pacific waters to lend Admiral Nimitz a much needed hand as the lines of operation got further and further away. The fall of Saipan, Tinian and Guam marked the end of the outer enemy defense on the road to the Philippines. For out here we have seen that all roads lead to Manila. Only in China has the war gone against us in 1944. And the relief of China depends on the securing of Luzon.

With the simultaneous landings on Palau and Morotai September 15th, the way was opened for the first of a series of punches in knocking the Japanese out of the Philippines. The surprise landings in Leyte in October and the halving of the Philippines by the Mindoro landings in December were still just preliminaries to the final blow which had to be swung against Luzon itself.

But before our landings were secure, the Japanese fleet had to be accounted for. This was accomplished in the two great naval battles of 1944. The first Battle of the Philippine Seas in June was an overwhelming victory for Task Force 58 and the carrier planes. The second Battle of the Philippine Seas was just as decisive, though more costly to us. In this October battle the Japanese learned the Americans were in the Philippines to stay.

The liberation of Luzon and Manila is rightly a part of the chain of events of 1944. In a year's time we have come a long way from Tarawa and Cape Gloucester. Now we are on the homestretch of over three years of hard fighting. After Luzon must come China and Tokyo.

Amen! until tomorrow.

On this operation we will be passing right through the Philippine Islands on a route that has now been well-traversed by the conquerors of Mindoro. We will probably not see many of the over 7,000 islands that go to make up the Philippines but we will be sailing near the larger ones: Samar, Leyte, Mindanao, Negros, Panay, Mindoro, and then Luzon.

We should enter Leyte Gulf on Saturday morning. To do so we pass between Dinagat and Homonhon Islands, which are under our control. Homonhon has the distinction of being the first island Magellan landed on when he became the official discoverer of the Philippines in 1521.

We will then turn south through Surigao Strait where one assault of the Japanese attack force in the second battle of the Philippine Sea was defeated. The small Surigao island is in our control. On our port side will be the second largest island, Mindanao, where the enemy expected our initial attack. On the starboard side will be Bohol and Negros as we pass through the Mindanao Sea.

Between these two islands is the thin island of Cebu where the first Spanish government was set up in the sixteenth century, even before the city of Manila was founded.

Skirting Negros we will turn north through the Sulu Sea, pass Panay, which you will remember was the name of the gunboat, sunk in China, December 12, 1937, by the Japanese, the cause of an international incident. It is possible that up until that time the Japanese will expect us to be reinforcing Mindoro. But we will bear northwest through the Mindoro Straits and enter the South China Sea. With a sweep around the Manila area we will arrive at our target on "Sugar" Day, one week from today.

We will have more to say about these separate islands as we pass by them. All of us realize that we will be deep in enemy-held territory. On many of the 7,000 islands there are no Japanese, and on enemy-held islands there are many friends of ours. A good thing to know in case we should really have to abandon ship.

The group of islands called Nanpo Shoto, meaning "southern islands" run directly south of Tokyo along the 140 meridian. They are slightly to the west of north from the Mariannas. The word "shoto" means a "large group of islands." Nanpo Shoto falls into three geographic groups: at the north, the Imu Islands; in the center the Ogasawaro Gunto or Bonin Islands; in the south, the Kazan Retto or Volcano Islands. The islands have no particular value except in the military sense. Many of them are uninhabited. As you may notice on your maps each has several names and several spellings.

The islands of Nanpo Shoto are Japanese in every respect. The people, the language, the customs are those of the Japanese homeland. The northern Izu group was settled first by a few fishermen. Beginning in 1601 they were used as a place of exile for political prisoners, sort of a Japanese Siberia.

The Bonins were discovered by a Japanese, Sadayou Ogasawara, in 1593. Because they were uninhabited, they were called "bonin," meaning "no men." Colonization failed. In 1823 an American whaler stopped at Haha Jima and claimed it as an American possession. Two years later an English ship visited Chichi Jima and claimed it. In 1828 the Russians put in their oar. (Sounds like they needed another Big Three conference.) The claims didn't get anywhere.

The first permanent settlers to arrive in the Bonins were a mixed group consisting of several Englishmen, Portuguese and Italians, seventeen Hawaiians and one American, Nathaniel Savory, from Massachusetts. These people stayed, claiming British sovereignty. But Commodore Perry, who visited Chichi Jima in 1853, proclaimed the islands rightfully belonged to Japan by right of Ogasawara's discovery. Commodore Perry bought, for the U.S., some land at Futami Ko, the harbor of Chichi Jima, to be used for a coaling station. Savory was appointed agent, but when the Commodore left, the project was dropped.

Japanese colonists came and went but Savory remained the top man on the islands. However, in 1875 the Japanese made formal claim to the Bonins, and by the time the British got through protesting, they were well established.

Savory and his companions stayed in the Bonins, intermarried with the Japanese and were allowed to settle there. Perhaps a few descendants of Savory and his companions know some English with a Boston accent, but otherwise the effect of their colonization was wiped out.

The Volcano Islands were discovered in 1543 by the Spaniard, Bernard de Torres, and then they were forgotten for 130 years. An Englishman, named Gore, visited the islands and called them the Sulphur Islands. Gore was followed in 1805 by the Russian explorer, Krusenstern. Spain claimed the islands but the claims were never backed up and not until the Japanese came in 1887 were there any colonists. By 1891 the Japanese had a firm grip on Kaza Retto, Volcano or Sulphur Islands (whatever you want to call them) and they incorporated them into the Bonin government administration.

Amen! until tomorrow.

The Pattern Forms   February 18, 1945

Today is D minus 1. H-hour is scheduled for 0900 tomorrow morning. At this point it is well to look at our target and evaluate its significance.

Since we gained control of the Marianas, Iwo Jima has been subject to constant bombardment by land-based planes as well as carrier planes and warships. But in spite of this pounding its proximity to Tokyo has enabled it to be resupplied. Planes have flown from here to raid the B-29 field at Saipan as well as attack B-29 waves in and out of the Empire. It has therefore been of nuisance value to the enemy. But it has a greater significance. We need these three airfields on Iwo for fighter planes to give protection to our B-29s from Saipan and Guam.

You can see how the pattern has formed. Simultaneously with the beginning of the bombardment on the island, Halsey's big, fast task force has kept the enemy airforce occupied in the main Honshu island or Tokyo area. B-29s have stepped up the intensity of their runs before, during and after the carrier force struck. Today the bombardment continues and Halsey's force will move south to cover the landings at Iwo, providing day and night fighter protection. Obviously, he still hopes that some units of the Japanese fleet will come out and fight.

Tomorrow the 4th Marine Division, who embarked at Maui, and the new and untried 5th Marine Division, who embarked at the big island of Hawaii, will land on beaches on the east coast. The 3rd Marine Division is in reserve and will land at D plus 1 or after if they are needed. The transports carrying the 4th and 5th are all new, this being their first operation.

The island of Iwo has a resemblance to South America in outline or it might remind you more of a ham hock. At its widest part it is only 2½ miles and its longest portion is 4½ miles. But don't let its size fool you. Betio island in Tarawa atoll was smaller still. But then Tarawa didn't get the pounding that Iwo has had, and another important difference, this beach is sand and not coral.

It is intended that Iwo be hit hard and fast and overrun as quickly as possible. This is the kind of work Marines are trained for and this is what they will undoubtedly do. We only hope the job will be such a pushover that the 3rd Division will not be called to land.

Amen! until tomorrow.

U.S.S. Frederick Funston (APA89)
February 18, 1945

CAPTAIN'S MESSAGE TO THE CREW
PRIOR TO THE INVASION OF IWO JIMA

This is the Captain.

Tomorrow is D-day for the assault on Iwo Jima. Although we are not scheduled to go in until D plus 1, we shall be well within the operating area and ready in all respects to proceed in case we are needed. You officers and men of the *Frederick Funston* have rehearsed the fundamentals, are fully capable of making an expeditious and well-executed landing under hazardous conditions, and possibly look upon this operation as "just another one of those things."

I hope, however, that you will bear in mind and appreciate the fact that conditions under which you operate become increasingly more difficult as we approach the Japanese Empire — now only 750 miles away — and that your hard earned lessons of previous invasions will not be forgotten. This attack will be quite similar to that launched at Saipan, only the island is smaller and a more concentrated mortar fire is to be expected. That you will complete the operation with courage and devotion to duty of the highest order, I do not doubt for one minute; you have proven this many times before.

I ask of you this — *do your duty to the best of your ability*, even though the task to be accomplished is a long and tedious one, and all will be successful in the end. If you continue to carry your share of the burden as heretofore, in the same excellent manner, the final outcome will bring us one step closer to victory. May God have mercy on your souls and protect you in the coming invasion.

Carry on.

C. C. Anderson

The First Inning   February 19, 1945

Yesterday underwater demolition squads encountered heavy artillery and mortar fire from the beaches. Heaviest fire came from the right flank and "Hot Rocks" on the southern tip. Two LCI's were hit with thirty-one dead and eighty-three wounded. One old destroyer was hit and one cruiser was hit in Batt II by coast defense artillery or heavy mortar, killing the executive officer.

From 0700 to 1830 yesterday four BBs and one CA delivered uninterrupted fire at short range on east beaches, with principal defenses believed destroyed or heavily damaged. AA fire has been varied but accurate with numerous planes damaged, but there have been no air personnel losses. Minesweeping was completed without results. No underwater obstacles were encountered. Grounded planes and barges were destroyed on nearby Chichi Jima and Haha Jima.

Landings were made at the scheduled 0900 this morning on the preferred beaches. The immediate objective was the large Motoyama airfield No. 1 but it was hoped that the line would secure all the southern end of the island by nightfall. From all reports we could pick up today, the 4th Division on the right flank, have reached the No. 1 airfield. No reports have come from the 5th Division on the left flank.

This is likely to be a rough night on the beaches. "Hot Rocks" on the left flank has turned out to be an exceptionally strong point. This is an isolated steep-sided, volcanic cone rising 554 feet at the southwest end of the island. It is like a tower controlling the land around. Mortars or hidden artillery from this sector combined with the inevitable Japanese night counterattacks can make a man lose a lot of sleep.

In the northern end of the island there has been a heavy concentration of AA fire in the vicinity of Moto Yama. This is the one and only town on the island, housing about 1,000 civilians. However, these civilians were probably evacuated months ago.

You probably noticed the pleasant change in temperature this morning. February is the coolest month in the year in this area. Average temperature is 62 degrees F. and temperatures rarely fall below 45 degrees F. This is also the dryest season with only 3½ inches reported. Actually we are in the same latitude as Key West, Florida, where the rich go to spend the winter.

If we get any official word tomorrow on the progress of the battle, you will be informed. Meanwhile tonight about 2200 we will be in the rendezvous area eighty miles off Iwo.

Amen! until tomorrow.

The news tonight is as good as we can expect although the reports are necessarily fragmentary. Our line extends clear across the island now and lies about 800 yards south of the 0-1 line. The right flank is in the vicinity of the quarry. All of airfield No. 1 has been taken except one small tip. The west beach is secured. Artillery fire is still falling on our beachhead. Severe air strikes have been made today against "Hot Rocks" and the northern area to eliminate this fire. One cave position on "Hot Rocks" is known to have been sealed. We have two artillery regiments now operating.

On this type of volcanic island there is bound to be numerous caves and holes, either made by nature or man. Against such, naval gunfire and air bombing is of little effect. The only way to clean out such positions as we learned in the Marianas and Peleliu is to take them one at a time and that is the work of the infantry. Naturally it will take time. But things must be going definitely in our favor or a call for reserves would have been made by this time.

Admiral Nimitz's announcement in the morning news spoke of this landing on Iwo Jima as the first against the Japanese homeland. This statement is justified on the basis that Iwo is and has always been occupied by the Japanese. Saipan, Tinian and Palau have only been Japanese since World War I when they seized them from the Germans. They were supposed to have been held in mandate from the League of Nations. Technically they never really belonged to Japan. But when Japan left the League she refused to relinquish the mandates and so can only be said to have stolen these islands. That is why Iwo becomes another "first" in the war and justified Admiral Nimitz's statement.

We had a first on the Freddy today also: i.e., our first "stowaway." It seems that a CB found Guam getting a bit too civilized so he joined the Marines without going through proper channels. Discovered at a map briefing yesterday by a Marine officer, he is now a P.A.L. and will undoubtedly fail to see the action he hoped for.

One of the artillery spotter planes was heard calling attention to an artillery emplacement today. In fact he called attention to it several times without any response. Finally he said sarcastically, "The least you can do is waste the price of a couple of war bonds on it."

Amen! until tomorrow.

February 21, 1945

Today the situation has changed somewhat. At the present time our line extends from the 0-1 line on the left flank to a point even with the lower end of airstrip No. 2. But around this end there is evidently heavy resistance for the line sags there and picks up on the other side to a point beyond the 0-1 line. This latter bulge is headed toward the highest observation point on the island, hill 382. With this in our hands we will have observation for artillery over any point on the northern end. It is possible that these two bulges will act as pincers over the resistance around airstrip No. 2.

Here is a message from Admiral Nimitz:

The officers and men of the first carrier task force of the Pacific Fleet have dealt the enemy a crushing blow which will long be remembered. The same courage and teamwork which enabled our carrier pilots to destroy the enemy in bad weather over Tokyo are now being displayed by the forces which are taking Iwo Island only 660 miles from Japan. They will bring success when our troops land in Japan itself covered and supported by the ever increasing power of our air forces and the guns of the fleet. To those brave officers and men who have been and are in combat and also to those whose support and assistance in rear areas are essential to their successes. Well done!

183

It might be added that the carrier force did such a good job, we have not heard of any enemy air raids over Iwo yet.

The Marines claim they have a new secret weapon in the attack on Iwo. What is it? *No Army.*

Amen! until tomorrow.

(see "The Anderson Story" on page 199)

The death of our Captain's son, Sgt. Charles Carter Anderson, Jr., USMC, on March 4th as a result of wounds received at Iwo Jima was deeply felt by all hands. The sympathy of the officers and men was expressed to Captain Anderson by the Chaplain and the following letter was sent to Mrs. Anderson.

15 March 1945

Mrs. Charles C. Anderson
3611 34th Street N.W.,
Washington 8, D.C.

Dear Mrs. Anderson,

The tragedy that has recently come into your home is shared by every officer and man of the U.S.S. *Frederick Funston*. It is on their behalf, as well as my own, that I extend our deepest sympathy to you.

For the past eight months many of us have become acquainted with Charles as he visited his father and the ship. He was welcome enough as the son of our Captain. But he soon became welcome among us for himself.

All hands knew Charles by sight and when he was brought aboard among the casualties he was cared for as tenderly as a brother. With all his serious injuries he retained his sense of humor and to the end never

184

complained about himself, thinking only of his father and the hardships of his buddies.

It was indeed fortunate that Chaplain James Finnigan was aboard at the time and could administer extreme unction and later to conduct a requiem mass. I offered prayer at the moment of death and at 1000 that morning we held a memorial service with the Captain present.

All honors possible were accorded to the body and I hope you will feel that the decision to lay him at rest with his buddies on Iwo Jima was the wisest under the circumstances.

One word must be added. We all admire the fine way our Captain has borne his grief. It helped us to understand how Charles bore his so well. We only hope and pray yours will be the same strength that was your son's and your husband's.

God be with you,

John D. Wolf
Chaplain, USNR

Gone But Not Forgotten   March 7, 1945

Our arrival off Apra Harbor at 0800 tomorrow will end the Freddy's seventh campaign. I am sure that in all our memories it will stand alone in its uniqueness and tragic nature.

At the beginning we thought it would be a "quick" run. It has taken us nearly three weeks. And what the marines believed could be, at worst, another Tarawa, Saipan, Peleliu has turned out to be without precedent. When the fighting finally ceases, Mt. Surabachi will stand like a giant tombstone over the graves of thousands of marines and a sandy desolation that has no comparison this side of hell.

185

If the Siegried line had been packaged up into a bundle 2½ by 4½ miles there would scarcely have been more defenses or more skillful ingenuity employed than at Iwo. The cream of our nation's fighting men are still over there digging them out of pillboxes one after another and this is D plus 17.

The question has arisen in many minds as to whether or not Iwo was worth it all. We can all agree that as far as real estate is concerned it is not worth one single American life. But in the total pattern of the war Iwo may prove to be the saving of many lives. With this, and the next Marine operation that will come later, the encirclement of the main islands of Japan by air bombardment and fighting power together with sea power, will be virtually complete. Such a pounding will continue until sufficient troops can be brought out into this area to launch landings on China or Japan proper. The place Iwo will play in these plans to bring Japan eventually to her knees will be very great.

Despite the fact that we did not land the 3rd Marines, the part we played in this operation is hardly insignificant. And the fact that one regiment could be spared from the fight is something to be very thankful for.

Probably this general review can best end in appreciation of the entire crew and the fine work of the medical officers and corpsmen, both Navy and marine, who have done such an excellent job in restoring the strength of our 180 casualties. It was truly a job well done!

"Considering all the uncertainties of this operation, I think Transport Division 33 did a bang up job."

Captain Haight, Commander TransDiv 33.

Amen! until tomorrow.

Going, Going, Guam   March 9, 1945

Tonight we shove off for Noumea, New Caledonia, with a stop at Tulagi and Guadalcanal, all of which are "down under." Distance to Tulagi (our first stop) is 1,837 miles and should take us about seven days.

It is too bad that most of you did not get a chance to look Guam over while we were here. Secretary Forrestal called Guam the "Times Square" of the Pacific and it is truly that. As the forward headquarters of Admiral Nimitz it has grown remarkably since we landed on it last July. Here are some of the sights around the island you might have seen.

Apra Harbor has had to be improved a great deal. Only one third of the blasting and dredging of the harbor that is to be done, is now complete. Large jetties and piers at Sumay have been made by dredging and filling in. For example, last night we docked at pier No. 1. To do so we went around a little jut of land with old ruins on it. This is the old fort Santa Cruz, built by the Spanish in 1670 and captured by us in 1898 without a fight. The fort once set on an island so that everything we saw from there had been filled in.

On Orote peninsula, where the hardest fighting for the Marines took place, is the large navy airfield and N.O.B. Down at Agat, where we landed the 77th, a completely new village has been built to house the natives. Here also is one of the three U.S. cemeteries.

The most amazing thing about Guam is the large number of four lane highways that have been built and paved from Agat, clear up to the bomber fields. You would think you were driving in California if it weren't for the many signs of war around.

The beach at Agat is still cluttered with wrecks of alligators and here and there along the reefs toward Agana are more wrecks sitting where they were hit. Every single house has been hit with the exception of one in the city of Agana. The town itself will have to be entirely rebuilt. The best houses have a red triangle on them denoting that Japanese officers were quartered there. The churches, the bank, schools and hospital were all wrecked in our bombardments. The once beautiful plaza in the center of town had been used by the Japanese as an open cesspool.

187

On the plateau above Agana is the Navy's air terminal, a beautiful new streamlined building. Casualties are being flown back to the states every day out of here. Not far distant is the big Army 21st Bomber command. Here the B-29s are parked and serviced. When they have all of the bomber fields completed there will be more B-29s flying out of Guam than out of Saipan.

After the island was announced as secured, several thousand more Japanese were killed. Patrols were constantly on the lookout for them. At one time the whole island was patrolled at once. But to kill them all is impossible in the jungle and ravines of the north. Several hundred are still at large and turn up now and then to steal food and supplies. One major has a radio that the Marines could listen in on but they have never located it. It is also possible that some of the enemy have seeped in from Rota. Prisoners are used as labor around the island.

Now that we are "Going, Going, Guam" from Guam we can turn our attention to other matters. We welcome aboard the new supply officer Lt.(jg) Arthur S. Gregory who will relieve Mr. Abbott. All hands had better start planning for another shellback initiation in the not too distant future.

A hearty "tare, victor, george" to Lt.(jg) Bill Downey who is largely responsible for obtaining our mail this afternoon, which had been missent to Saipan.

* * *

Iwo was announced as secured on March 16, 1945. Casualties were over 20,000 and dead over 4,100.

Time magazine for March 5th made the following statement in regard to Iwo.

> *Last week, as the Battle for Iwo raged in fury, the nation learned what force of arms, character and courage meant. No battle of World War II, not even Normandy, was watched with more intensity by the U.S. people. Everyone knew Iwo's strategic importance, and everyone sensed that casualties would be high.*

Iwo held top place in the minds and hearts of Americans. Henceforth, Iwo would be a place name in U.S. history to rank with Valley Forge, Gettysburg and Tarawa. Few in this generation would ever forget Iwo's shifting black sands, or the mind's images of charging Marines, or the sculptured picture of Old Glory rising atop Mount Suribachi on February 24th.

Amen! until tomorrow.

The Carolines Again   March 11, 1945

At the present time we are passing through the Caroline Islands. All of these islands except Angaur, Peleliu and Ulithi are in enemy hands. You will recall that on our trip from Eniwetok to Manus the first time, we passed between Ponape and Kusaie. This time the nearest atoll of any consequence that we pass is Woleai, twenty-five miles off the port beam at 0500.

All of these island providing harbors and water were once haunts of the whalers for one of the best whaling fields was between the Marianas and the Carolines. Woleai is halfway between Truk and Palau and provides an anchorage and land and seaplane landing areas. It is about five and a half miles along, three miles wide, and fifteen miles in circumference. It is a typical atoll, similar to others in the Gilberts, Marshalls and Carolines.

The people of the islands are usually short, slender and lithe. Their color is light brown and their hair is dark brown or black. Noses and mouths are large. After their youth is passed the native women become too plump for American standards of beauty.

We will cross the equator about noon Tuesday at approximately the same longitude that we crossed it the first time.

Amen! until tomorrow.

189

March 12, 1945

"By special communication His Majesty has indicated his intention to hold regal ceremony doctrine the forenoon of 13 March. Royal subjects of His Majesty King Neptune will be expected to render full honors and courtesies to his majesty during his visit. All Episoctic life such as Polliwogs will be properly prepared for His Majesty's visit."

Signed:
Davey Jones.

The Solomon Islands   March 14, 1945

Last December we crossed the Bismarck Sea twice going to New Britain. On this trip we are going down the east coast of the Bismarck Archipelago, passing New Hanover and New Ireland today before reaching the Solomon Islands. These former islands are still in enemy hands as is the eastern end of New Britain. The formerly important bases of Kavieng on New Ireland and Rabaul on New Britain have been by-passed by the fast moving war.

For every American the name Solomon Islands marks the site of important land and naval battles in which the enemy found that at last he had reached a limit to his stolen empire. Tomorrow we will be opposite the first of the Solomons, Bougainville, also the largest of the group. The islands lie in a double chain stretching 720 miles from southeast by east to northwest by west. There are ten large islands and twenty secondary islands all totally about 15,000 square miles.

Bougainville and the islands at the north are under Australian mandate from the League of Nations. The rest of the islands are a British Protectorate since 1893 administered from Suva, Fiji. Most of the islands are mountainous, heavily wooded and well watered. Before the war the entire group held about 500 Europeans, 200 Chinese and 95,000 natives, most of whom were on Bougainville and Malaita.

The two islands of the Solomons that we will be most interested in are Guadalcanal and Florida Islands. Tulagi, the capital of the entire Solomon group, lies twenty-two miles to the north of Guadalacanal on a tiny island of its own so situated just off the shore of Florida Island as to create the finest harbor in the archipelago.

Guadalcanal is the second largest island in the Solomons. The island is formed by a sunken mountain of which it is the peak. It is ninety-two miles long and thirty-three miles wide at the widest part. It is very rugged and rises at places to 8,000 feet. Harbors are few and Tulagi acts as the harbor for the entire group. Because of the separating nature of terrain there are twenty dialects spoken on Guadalcanal. On the north coast there is enough level land however to have an airfield, thus explaining the strategic importance of the bloody battleground.

Florida island is twenty-two miles long and three to four miles wide. If it was not for Tulagi it could hardly be considered important. Tulagi island itself is only three miles in circumference. On it was the village of Tulagi where the small but attractive government buildings were located. Here were the few signs of civilization in the islands before the war. A few telephones and an ice plant and the regular steamer from Sydney, made the port the "New York" of the Solomons.

The climate in this vicinity is not healthful and malaria, dengue fever and dysentery abound. Rainfall is 160 inches per year. This month marks the change of the seasons.

The Solomons are an anthropologist's happy hunting grounds. Here are found the most primitive forms of man in different stages of development. The natives are all Melanesians but much mixture is evident. They are — or until recently have been — cannibals. Osa Johnson in her book "Bride in the Solomons," has actually photographed the natives eating human flesh. Headhunting is still not uncommon, British government agencies and missions have made some progress with them.

Villages are crude with a devil house surrounded by carved and burnt-out wooden figures. The natives chew betel nut and slit their ears to carry objects of considerable size.

Amen! until tomorrow.

Iron Bottom Bay   March 15, 1945

It was just one year ago tomorrow that we arrived in Honolulu for the first time. It was just six months ago today that we left Honolulu for the last time. Besides being the Ides of March, the day the income tax is due, and pay day, there is little else we can add to our log. Tomorrow about 1300 we arrive in Tulagi harbor where we expect to get a few new boats and, though we are ahead of the mail schedule, we hope to receive mail. We will only be there one day.

To cover the military events of the Solomons we have to go back nearly three years to April 1942 when the Japanese had established bases in this area, thus threatening all Melanesia and Australia. On May 3rd the Japanese began to occupy Florida Island and the next day the task force under Rear Admiral F. J. Fletcher composed of the *Yorktown*, *Astoria*, *Chester* and *Portland* and six DDs launched the opening round of the Navy's battle. A number of enemy vessels were sunk and damaged in Tulagi harbor. Then two task units with the *Minneapolis*, *New Orleans*, *Astoria*, *Chester* and *Portland* in one, the *Australia*, *Hobart*, *Chicago*, *Lexington* and *Yorktown* in the other, prepared to repel enemy amphibious landings against Port Moresby. We lost the *Lexington*, the tanker *Neosho* and DD *Sims*, sixty-six planes and 543 men in this action but the Japanese advance was checked and she lost even more.

The Coral Sea engagement marked the end of the totally defensive period. Then, while the Battle of Midway was fought, both sides got ready for further blows, this time with us in the offensive.

192

On August 7th the landing force composed of Marines, took the enemy by surprise, made landings on Guadalcanal and Tulagi. By the next morning the Marines were in complete control of Tulagi and were making satisfactory progress on Guadalcanal, where they had taken possession of the airfield. We lost one transport and one DD in this operation.

On August 9th the Japanese launched a surprise night attack on our naval force protecting the landings. In the resulting Battle of Savo Island we lost the *Vincennes*, *Quincy*, *Astoria* and *Canberra*. The *Yorktown* having been lost at Midway we were at a serious weakness. Fortunately the Japanese did not know this and did not launch a full naval attack. They did bomb Guadalcanal by day and shelled it at night, running the "Tokyo Express" down the "slot" and around Savo Island.

On August 24th the Battle of the Eastern Solomons began and we stopped an attempted reinforcement of Guadalcanal. Later we lost the *Wasp* and five DDs trying to keep the supply lines open. The next Battle of Cape Esperance, at the northern end of Guadalcanal, was a defeat for the Japanese and a tactical surprise. But in two months the enemy had landed two new divisions on the "Canal" and by October 25-26 launched their strongest offensive with naval support.

The enemy force thus engaged in the Battle of Santa Cruz Island was stopped but we lost the *Hornet* and one DD. To recite all the engagements in this area would take more time than we have tonight. The Battle of Guadalcanal was fought November 13-15 in violent action as both sides attempted to land reinforcements. We lost the *Atlanta* and *Juneau* in winning this battle. On November 30 we again stopped an attempt by the enemy to reinforce Guadalcanal and in this action we lost the *Northampton*. February 7-8, 1943, the Japanese withdrew from the Canal. The loss of all these ships together with a greater number of enemy ships in the waters between Guadalcanal, Savo and Florida has given it the name "iron bottom bay". It was the decisive turning point in the war that put us from the defensive to the offensive though at the cost of many ships.

To the Marines of the 5th Amphibious Corps and to all
the supporting forces I send my admiration and congratu-
lations on an achievement that brings this war much
closer to the inevitable end. In capturing Iwo which is
as important as it was tough you have overcome the most
difficult defenses that skill and ingenuity could construct
on a small island that nature herself had already made
strong for military defense.

Your victory which was assured almost from the first
landing will brighten the pages of American history. To-
day your fellow countrymen humbly and profoundly sing
your praises.   Admiral Nimitz

Amen! until tomorrow.

The Coral Sea   March 19, 1945

There was not a great deal to observe in our short stay at
Tulagi, Florida and Lunga Point, Guadalcanal. What was once
the crossroads of the south Pacific and the staging area for
campaigns in the New Guinea area, is rapidly becoming a ghost
base of haunted memories. It is likely that we will find Noumea, which was once Admiral Halsey's South Pacific fleet
headquarters, also practically deserted.

We are now, for the first time, in the Coral Sea. It was
nothing new for the "Freddy" to be at Guadalcanal for she
made her maiden voyage there as an Army transport over two
years ago. But Noumea will be the furthest south we will go.
We will be about 22°S which is about the same latitude as Key
West, Florida and Iwo Jima is north. We are going west of
the New Hebrides at the present time and will come into Noumea from the west.

If you saw the picture "Pardon My Sarong" last night,
any description of New Caledonia would be superfluous. With
that picture of the South Seas in your mind you will find the
following a bit drab.

194

You will be interested to know that Noumea is closer to Pearl Harbor and the States than is Guam. Guadalcanal is closer than either. It is only 800 miles from Brisbane, Australia and a little over 1,000 miles to Auckland, New Zealand.

New Caledonia is a very large island, 250 miles long and thirty-six miles wide. It runs northwest-southeast. It is mountainous and has sixteen rivers. Compared to the Solomons the islands will look bare, but palms will be found near the beaches. She is rich in minerals, especially nickel.

We will find the climate healthful and not particularly hot. The island is kind of a half-breed between the tropics and Australia, New Zealand.

The people are Melanesians though of mixed blood. There are 51,000 of them and over 11,000 of these live in Noumea, plus some Europeans. The natives have a peculiar beehive shaped hut and wear little clothing. They dislike work, especially for wages. In counting they can only go up to five. Ten is thus "two fives" and twenty is "man." This apparently comes from the number of man's fingers and toes.

Their best native work is carving and decoration. Women tatoo themselves and both sexes pierce the lobes of their ears.

I'll tell you more about Noumea tomorrow night. We should arrive Wednesday noon.

Amen! until tomorrow.

Noumea: Furthest South   March 20, 1945

Our old friend Captain Cook discovered New Caledonia in 1774. The coast was explored thoroughly twenty years after by two Frenchmen d'Entrecasteaux and de Kerma dec. For the next half century the island was a refuge for seamen, for runaway convicts from New South Wales, and for fortune hunters. In 1853 the French government stepped in after the crew of a French survey ship had been killed and eaten on the island. It has been French ever since.

France set up a penal settlement there in 1864 but the last native uprisings were not put down until 1881. The native appetite for white men could not be downed so easily however. In 1917 a native chief led an attack on a white settlement and ate some of his victims. The island has been fairly peaceful ever since after vigorous measures were adopted.

Area for area New Caledonia has the richest mineral resources in the world. Next to Canada, it is the world's most important source of nickel. Chrome, cobalt, manganese, zinc and antimony are also important. At least Japan thought so for she needed these minerals badly and long ago sent miners and traders there as well as machinery to control the exportation. The French colony was Free French however and strongly pro-Ally. When they took over they clamped down on all Japanese interests.

Noumea itself is the administrative center of all French possessions in this part of the world. It is one of the largest towns in the South Pacific.

Lying on an exceptionally fine harbor, created by a three-mile island which lies across the sea side of a triangular indentation in the coast, Noumea is flat and laid out in square blocks, the streets running parallel. The town was once hot, dusty and unattractive, but the planting of coconut palms and other trees along the streets and in the central square has greatly improved its comfort and appearance. Most structures are one story in height and most of them are of wood with tin roofs. The Cathedral, however, which is east of the town on hills that slope up, is the more striking because of the low buildings in town. Pan-American Airways have a seaplane base on the island.

Here is the way one navy officer wrote of entering Noumea:

> We stood through the barrier reef toward Noumea, with Amedee Island light on its gleaming coral base framed against the blue-gray towering hills of New Caledonia. The tourist trade hawkers can rave about Waikiki and the Riviera, but for me there's no bit of scenic beauty that can compare with the reef-line North Bulari Passage guarded by that delightful sentinel, Amedee Island.

We passed through the picturesque entrance to Great Roads, and dropped the hook inside. As usual, there was a spinal meningitis epidemic in Noumea, so there could be no liberty for the crew.

This was written several years ago so whether there is a spinal meningitis epidemic there now or whether there is any liberty are questions that will have to wait until we get in. At least there should be mail and fleet recreation. We will be there about ten days. Our reason for coming here, incidentally, is to pick up Army reserves for the next operation.

The "Freddy" has traveled a total of 70,800 miles since she was commissioned. Forty-nine thousand and sixty-six of these miles were in the Pacific.

Tonight's broadcast is 100th since we began last May 30th.

Amen, until the next Chaplain and, —

God Bless You!

The Anderson Story

On February 19, 1945, at 0900, Marines landed on the beaches of Iwo Jima. The *Funston* was carrying the 3rd Marine Division to be in reserve.

On March 3rd I was on the bridge when the "skipper," Captain Charles Carter Anderson, USN, received a message from the flagship, hurriedly ordered his gig, and sped to a nearby ship that was taking on casualties. Searching the stretchers waiting to be hoisted aboard, he passed over one when he heard "Hey, Dad." Beneath the wounds he hadn't recognized his only son, Sgt. Charles Carter Anderson, Jr., USMC, 4th Division.

Carter's wounds were extensive. His unit had been moving up the eastern shore of the tiny island but were in reserve, some distance behind the front lines. An enemy mortar landed on a land mine and exploded close to Carter. The shrapnel cut off both his legs, the right one below the knee and the left above the knee. His right arm was so punctured that amputation would be necessary and the left arm was a mass of torn flesh. He had serious head wounds over the right eye and numerous minor wounds. Carter had enough consciousness to ask to be taken to his father's ship.

A few days before, on D plus 8, I had seen a soot-covered Marine coming up the gangway. After eight days under heavy fire, Carter had seen his dad's ship with her large APA 89 on the bow, anchored off shore, and somehow had finagled permission to visit. It was a welcome reunion for father and son, a quick shower, a steak dinner and then back to duty.

Carter and I had become well acquainted back in Pearl Harbor when opportunity provided for visits to the *Funston*. We had played chess, talked about his life at Georgetown University, interrupted by his enlistment February 12, 1943, at the age of nineteen. He impressed me as very intelligent and anxious to complete his education.

Then came Saipan, where Captain Anderson assumed command of the "Fighting Freddy." By way of the Navy grapevine he had discovered that his son's unit was also to be engaged in that battle. The *Funston* carried the 2nd Marines and Carter was in the 4th. At the final rendezvous point (Eniwetok), the two had met and Carter had had a chance to visit his father's new command. "Is she a snazzie ship!" he had written home to his mother. Since fresh water showers for Marines were unknown at sea, Carter wrote, "I had a shave and took two showers."

A few days after the landings on Saipan on June 15, 1944, and just before he assumed command of the *Funston*, the skipper had invited me to go ashore with him to search for his son. He suggested I strap on a 45 automatic (for which I had qualified at Newport, although chaplains are noncombatants and do not carry arms). We got in the captain's gig and headed for the beaches on the west side and south of the capital city of Garapan. Here he commandeered a jeep and headed for the Aslito airfield. Intelligence information indicated that Carter's unit had moved up to the north. We returned to the ship where we learned later that Carter had been wounded and evacuated to another ship. It seems the Marines were detonating caves in which the enemy were hiding, and a large rock had exploded, hitting Carter in the back. Word was he was not seriously hurt. Later when the *Funston* unloaded its 200 casualties at Pearl, Carter had been able to visit his dad's ship several times.

But this time Carter knew his wounds were fatal. To survive would have left him a quadruple paraplegic. Conscious most of the night, he cracked jokes with those who tended his wounds. To his dad he said, "This is one way to get aboard your ship." Trying to clean the volcanic ash off his face, he cracked, "Hey, doc, those lips are sunburned, take it easy." He apologized, "Don't let it worry you if have to throw up. I had some "J" (Japanese) fish for lunch."

Because of the danger from Kamikaze suicide planes, ships at Iwo got underway before darkness and returned to continue unloading and receiving casualties at dawn. Since Carter was rational throughout the night, Captain Anderson came down frequently from the bridge to talk. It was during this time I learned Carter was Roman Catholic. His father was Protestant and was always in his place on the front row during divine services. I contacted Chaplain James Finnigan, a Catholic priest who was with the troops on board, and last rites were given. Ship's doctors Barrett, Brooks, Osborne, and Bryer, as well as Marine doctors, attended Carter along with the other 180 casualties we had aboard.

From time to time Carter seemed to rally. He asked about "playing golf with one arm" and "I wonder how mother will take this?" But the shock was too great to his body and he died at 9:45 a.m. on March 4th.

The entire *Funston* complement knew Carter from his frequent visits and word spread quickly about his death. Memorial services were held on board with all hands not on duty attending. Chaplain Finnigan and I then took the body ashore while the fighting was still raging on the north side of Iwo. The now famous flag-raising occurred on Mt. Suribachi on February 28th (D plus 8) and was visible from the 4th Division cemetery where we saw the body interred in grave number 1,013, 13th grave in the 21st row.

Carter's body, along with all buried on Iwo Jima, was later moved to the states. His body was reinterred April 14, 1948, in Arlington National Cemetery in section 12, grave number 5,761.

The circumstances and coincidences pertaining to Sgt. Anderson's death were unusual enough to be mentioned in *Time* magazine, to be the subject of a television program called *Navy Log*, and mentioned in the book *Iwo Jima* by Richard Newcomb.

I was so impressed by the heroic way in which Carter faced affliction and death, together with the affection I felt for Captain Anderson, I wrote on that March 4th in a letter to my wife Carolyn, "If we are ever blessed with another son, with your permission, I would like to name him Carter Anderson

Wolf." Our second son was born March 9th, 1946 and on Mother's Day, Captain Anderson and his wife Viola were sponsors to his baptism at Old North Methodist Church in Evansville, Indiana, by Dr. Frank Hamilton.

On November 22, 1982, with full military honors, Admiral Charles Carter Anderson was buried at Arlington. On October 20, 1984, his dear wife Viola's ashes were also laid to rest there, within sight of Carter's grave. I was privileged in both instances to put on the old blues and conduct the services. They are survived by adopted daughters Jeanne and Guinevere Anderson-Greist of Washington, D.C.

John D. Wolf

Epilogue

After the atomic bombing of Hiroshima and Nagasaki in 1945, Albert Einstein is reported to have said, "Everything has changed except our way of thinking."

My thinking about war began to change at Iwo Jima. I suppose it was partly the effect of burying dozens of fine young men at sea off the fantail or hauling their weighted bodies out to the edge of the reef and committing their bodies to the deep. At Iwo I took the body of Carter Anderson ashore for burial in the black volcanic ash (later all Iwo burials were reinterred, Carter's to Arlington). The "just war theory" that had led me to leave the safety of the pastorate for the battles of the Pacific, had seemingly been justified. The armed might of the United States and of our Allies had successfully destroyed the ambitious world view of Adolf Hitler and of the Japanese Empire. Who could say that the price in millions of lives and trillions of dollars in property was not worth it? Freedom had vanquished totalitarianism. It was a justified war.

Naming our second son after Sgt. Anderson was to be a reminder of the price paid in order that we might live. But now a more terrifying menace had arisen in the world — nuclear capabilities. Since World War II we have lived with nuclear deterrence while the Cold War build-up to 50,000 weapons of potential annihilation continued. Hiroshima has been multiplied over a million fold and the spread of nuclear capability has put the power to destroy planet earth in the hands of a number of third world nations. Any small war could accelerate into nuclear holocaust. Historians may argue "that the dropping of the atomic bombs ushering us into the new age, may have been the great blunder of history." (Cousins) It is not encouraging that on the eve of the 50th Anniversary of World War II, "fifty percent of Americans believe that a third worldwide war is a certainty." If that insanity should occur, scientists, church leaders and statesmen agree, it will be the end of Creation.

It was Norman Cousins, former editor of *Saturday Review*, who writes that we have until the end of the century to turn around the problems that will determine the future of the human race. Nuclear arms, hunger and poverty, and environmental deterioration are today's three horses of the apocalypse, according to Cousins.

In recent years in church sermons and in lectures at Valparaiso University, I have re-examined the presuppositions that led to the messages of *Amen! Until Tomorrow*. For myself, I have exorcised the ghostly myths of World War II. The first myth is that "war is winnable," like a football game. No more. The second myth is that "war can be moral." Right and wrong seemed clear in World War II although later developments in Japan and West Germany make us wonder "who won?" Certainly the crisis problems listed by Cousins cannot be settled by war. In fact they would likely be so global, we would be pushed over the brink of survival. The third myth is that we can go on spending for war without bankrupting the future. Already the cracks in the world economy, largely due to the build-up of expensive armament and past or present wars, threaten not only the large powers, but most of the third world nations. This makes for the conclusion that WAR itself is SIN. The Christian churches have gone through periods of Pacifism (the first centuries), Just Wars (Augustine) and Crusades. In the Nuclear Age there is no other conclusion for this writer, who affirms the need for limited use of force in the social order, than to affirm a sort of Nuclear pacifism.

Recent changes in the international scene as tensions are reduced and the Great Powers move towards disarming, together with the retreat of totalitarianism, bodes well for our future sanity. The challenge to the new generation is "Peacemaking," the cooperating with God's gift of Shalom. We must learn how to live on a shrinking planet with our enemies, even if we cannot love them. The science of conflict resolution can move into the forefront and usurp the power and importance of war preparation. The converting of bomb factories to useful peace time production will mean a great sacrifice and demand imagination and dedication. The billions of dollars dedicated to research and development of Star Wars and Stealth bombers, can be redirected to useful service of the human race. This former chaplain sees God's hand in this, just as God was present in the battles of the "Fighting Freddy." Perhaps the recall of these chapters of history will help us do what Einstein preached, "change our way of thinking." Mine has. It all began in the sands of Iwo Jima.

John D. Wolf

NOTE: A number of medals, citations, and commendations were made to officers and men on the *Funston*. Because I do not have a complete list, I can only list those reported to me.

Dr. Peter Brooks for care of the wounded.
John William Chancey, BM2c,
William Keith Hales, S1c,
Paul Francis Jacob, MoMM2c, for saving their broached boat in heavy surf at Iwo Jima.
My apologies to other shipmates who deserve recognition.

JDW

THE SECRETARY OF THE NAVY
WASHINGTON

The Secretary of the Navy takes pleasure in commending

LIEUTENANT JOHN DEMING WOLF, CHAPLAIN CORPS
UNITED STATES NAVAL RESERVE

for service as set forth in the following

CITATION:

"For outstanding performance of duty as Chaplain, attached to the U.S.S. FREDERICK FUNSTON, during five major assaults against the enemy at Salerno, Saipan, Guam, Leyte and Lingayen Gulf, from September 9, 1943, to January 10, 1945, and in five turn-about echelons. Valiant and courageous, Lieutenant Wolf brought the comfort of religion to those about to engage in battle, and himself set a splendid example of steadfastness and hope. Unmindful of his own safety, he followed the troops ashore during invasions to render assistance wherever it was needed and reported his observations to those who remained aboard ship. After each invasion, Lieutenant Wolf administered to the wounded, bringing them solace and constantly inspiring both Army and Navy personnel. His untiring energy and devotion to duty were in keeping with the highest traditions of the United States Naval Service."

A copy of this citation has been made a part of Lieutenant Wolf's official record, and he is hereby authorized to wear the Commendation Ribbon.

James Forrestal

Secretary of the Navy

Eternal Father, Strong to Save

MELITA 88.88.88.

WILLIAM WHITING, 1825-1878

JOHN B. DYKES, 1823-1876

1. E - ter - nal Fa - ther, strong to save, Whose arm hath bound the
2. O Christ, whose voice the wa - ters heard, And hushed their rag - ing
3. O Ho - ly Spir - it, who didst brood Up - on the wa - ters
4. O Trin - i - ty of love and power, Our bre-thren shield in

rest - less wave, Who bidst the might - y o - cean deep
at thy word, Who walk - edst on the foam - ing deep,
dark and rude; And bid their an - gry tu - mult cease,
dan - ger's hour; From rock and tem - pest, fire and foe,

Its own ap - point - ed lim - its keep: O hear us when we
And calm a - mid the storm didst sleep: O hear us when we
And give, for wild con - fu - sion, peace: O hear us when we
Pro - tect them where-so - e'er they go: Thus ev - er-more shall

cry to thee For those in per - il on the sea.
cry to thee For those in per - il on the sea.
cry to thee For those in per - il on the sea.
rise to thee Glad hymns of praise from land and sea. A-men.

The Navy Hymn sung at all divine services. (Courtesy of Armed
Forces Chaplain Board)

Glossary

AKA	Attack Cargo Amphibious
APA	Attack Transport Amphibious
BB	Battleship
CA	Cruiser
CL	Light Cruiser
CV	Carrier
CVE	Carrier Escort
DD	Destroyer
DE	Destroyer Escort
PT	Patrol Torpedo Boat — "Green Dragons"

All amphibious landing craft begin with (L)

LCI	Landing Craft Infantry
LCM	Landing Craft Mechanized
LCVP	Landing Craft Vehicle-Personnel
LCT	Landing Craft Tank
LSD	Landing Ship Dock
LSM	Landing Ship Mechanized
LST	Landing Ship Tank
LVT	Landing Vehicle Tank — "Water Buffalos"

CBs	Navy Construction Battalions
GQ	General Quarters
Davit	Pairs of cranes used to hoist and lower boats
Scuttlebutt	Rumor. Also refers to drinking fountains
Poggybait	Marine term for candy
HMS	His or Her Majesty's Ship
USS	United States Ship

U.S.S. Frederick Funston Itinerary

1- 24 April 1943 U.S.S. *Frederick Funston* commissioned as US Naval Vessel. Todd Shipyard, Hoboken, N.J. Time: 1300

2- 1 May, 1943 Departed New York, New York
2 May, 1943 Anchored Hampton Roads, VA. (first trip)   150.0

3- 12 May to 24 May 1943 Held training exercises in the Chesapeake Bay area (distance traveled estimated)   700.0

4- 8 June 1943 Departed Hampton Roads VA. (45th Inf. Div. embarked)
22 June 1943 Anchored Mers El Kebir Harbor, Algeria   4231.5

5- 24 June 1943 Departed Oran Harbor. Held training exercises for 45th Div. and returned 25 June. Place, Arzew   50.0

6- 5 July 1943 Departed Oran Harbor (45th Div. embarked)
10 July 1943 Anchored at Gela Gulf, Sicily (invasion)   1057.0

7- 13 July 1943 Departed Gela Gulf, Sicily
16 July 1943 Moored Jules Giraud Mole, Oran   801.0

8- 3 Aug. to 8 Aug. 1943 Trained 34th Div. at La Andualusai for Salerno invasion   60.0

9- 5 Sept. 1943 Departed Oran Harbor (36th Div. embarked)
9 Sept. 1943 Anchored Salerno Gulf, Italy (invasion) 883.0

10- 10 Sept. 1943 Departed Salerno Gulf, Italy
14 Sept. 1943 Moored Mers El Kebir Harbor   884.5

11- 19 Sept. 1943 Departed Oran Harbor (100th Batt, 34th Div.)
22 Sept. 1943 Anchored Salerno Gulf, Italy   840.0

12- 23 Sept. 1943 Departed Salerno Gulf, Italy
26 Sept. 1943 Moored Mers El Kebir Harbor   873.3

13- 7 Oct. 1943 Departed Mers El Kebir Harbor (service troops)
10 Oct. 1943 Anchored in Pozzuoli Gulf, Italy   867.3

14- 11 Oct. 1943 Departed Gulf of Pozzuoli, Italy
14 Oct. 1943 Moored Mers El Kebir Harbor   897.5

15-25 Oct. 1943 Departed Mers El Kebir (Engineers embarked)
28 Oct. 1943 Anchored in Gulf of Pozzuoli, Italy   896.5
16-28 Oct. 1943 Departed Gulf of Pozzuoli
31 Oct. 1943 Morred Mers El Kebir Harbor   891.0
17-14 Nov. 1943 Departed Oran Harbor (Amgot,
 Rangers, Service)
17 Nov. 1943 Moored to Mole Naples, Italy   886.5
18-19 Nov. 1943 Departed Naples, Italy (82nd Airborne
 embarked)
22 Nov. 1943 Moored Mers El Kebir Harbor   877.0
19-30 Nov. 1943 Departed Oran Harbor (82nd embarked)
9 Dec. 1943 Moored to dock Belfast, Ireland   2671.0
20-10 Dec. 1943 Departed Belfast Harbor
10 Dec. 1943 Anchored in Gourock Bay, Scotland   91.0
21-20 Dec. 1943 Departed Gourock Bay, Scotland
31 Dec. 1943 Anchored in Gravesend Bay, New York   3111.0
22- 1 Jan. 1944 Departed Gravesend Bay
1 Jan. 1944 Arrived Bethlehem Steel Shipyard   13.0

TOTAL NUMBER OF MILES TRAVELED FROM DATE OF COMMISSION
APRIL 24TH 1943 UNTIL DRYDOCKING IN SHIPYARD 1 JAN. 1944
21,734.3

23-19 Feb. 1944 Departed Bayonne, NJ
20 Feb. 1944 Arrived Davisville, RI   150.0
24-24 Feb. 1944 Departed Davisville, RI (129th CB's embarked)
25 Feb. 1944 Anchored Hampton Roads, VA   293.0
25-26 Feb. 1944 Departed Hampton Road, VA (129th
 CB's embarked)
2 Mar. 1944 Anchored Cristolbal Panama,
 Breakwater   1889.0
26- 2 Mar. 1944 Departed Cristobal Breakwater
2 Mar. 1944 Arrived and moored Dock 6, Balboa   50.0
27- 4 Mar. 1944 Departed Balboa
16 Mar. 1944 Moored to Dock Honolulu, TH   4859.0
28-From April 5, 1944 to April 27, 1944 two training runs
 Completed for 27th Inf. Division.   1744.0

29- 31 May 1944 Departed Pearl Harbor (2nd Mar Div. embarked)
  9 June 1944 Anchored Eniwetok Lagoon, Marshall Is.   2633.0
30- 11 June 1944 Departed Eniwetok Lagoon (2nd Mar Div. embarked)
  15 June 1944 Arrived transport area Saipan Is., Mariana Is.   1106.0
31- 15 June to 17 June 1944 Night retirement   284.0
32- 18 June 1944 Departed Saipan for fueling area
  21 June 1944 Arrived transport area Saipan   1117.0
33- 23 June 1944 Departed Saipan (Capt. C. C. Anderson relieved Capt. J. E. Murphy)
  3 July 1944 Arrived docks Honolulu, T.H.   3417.0
34- 8 July 1944 Departed Honolulu (77th Div. embarked)
  17 July 1944 Anchored Eniwetok Lagoon   2406.0
35- 18 July 1944 Departed Eniwetok Lagoon (77th Div.)
  22 July 1944 Arrived transport area Guam Is., Mariana, Is.   1078.0
36- 22 July 1944 to 27 July 1944 Night retirement
37- 28 July 1944 Departed Guam Island
  1 Aug. 1944 Anchored Eniwetok Lagoon   1189.0
38- 1 Aug. 1944 Departed Eniwetok Lagoon
  9 Aug. 1944 Anchored Pearl Harbor, T.H.   2546.0
39- 1 Sept. 1944 Departed Pearl Harbor, T.H.
  2 Sept. 1944 Arrived Maui, Island, T.H.   185.0
40- 3 & 4 Sept. 1944 Training at Kahoolawe, T.H. (Hilo) and around Maui, Island (96th Inf. Div. embarked)   379.0
41- 6 Sept. 1944 Departed Maui, Island
  7 Sept. 1944 Moored dock Honolulu, T.H.   190.0
42- 15 Sept. 1944 Departed Honolulu (96th Div. embarked)
  26 Sept. 1944 Anchored Eniwetok Lagoon   2471.0
43- 28 Sept. 1944 Departed Eniwetok Lagoon (96th Div.)
  3 Oct. 1944 Anchored Seeadler Harbor, Manus Is.   1440.0
44- 14 Oct. 1944 Departed Seeadler Harbor (96th Div.)
  20 Oct. 1944 Arrived transport area Leyte Is., Philippines   1552.0

45- 22 Oct. 1944 Departed Island of Leyte
27 Oct. 1944 Anchored Harbor of Hollandia, Dutch
New Guinea 1284.0
46- 30 Oct. 1944 Departed Hollandia
31 Oct. 1944 Anchored Harbor Aitape, New Guinea 120.0
47- 1 Nov. 1944 Departed Aitape Harbor (112th Cavalry embarked)
1 Nov. 1944 Arrived Hollandia 110.0
48- 2 Nov. 1944 Departed Hollandia (112th Cavalry)
5 Nov. 1944 Anchored Harbor Morotai, Is. 813.0
49- 10 Nov. 1944 Departed Morotai Island (112th Cavalry)
13 Nov. 1944 Anchored Leyte Gulf 1111.0
50- 14 Nov. 1944 Departed Leyte Gulf
20 Nov. 1944 Anchored Seeadler Harbor, Manus Is. 1558.0
51- 27 Nov. 1944 Departed Seeadler Harbor
28 Nov. 1944 Anchored Borgen Bay, New Britain 234.0
52- 10 Dec. 1944 Departed Borgen Bay (40th Div. embarked)
11 Dec. 1944 Anchored Seeadler Harbor 270.0
53- 16 Dec. 1944 Departed Seeadler Harbor (40th Div.)
18 Dec. 1944 Anchored in Huon Gulf (training exercises) 542.0
54- 19 Dec. 1944 Departed Huon Gulf
21 Dec. 1944 Anchored Seeadler Harbor 433.0
55- 31 Dec. 1944 Departed Seeadler Harbor (40th Div.)
9 Jan. 1944 Anchored Lingayen Gulf, Philippines 2366.0
56- 10 Jan. 1944 Departed Lingayen Gulf
13 Jan. 1944 Anchored Leyte Gulf 834.0
57- 19 Jan. 1944 Departed Leyte Gulf
23 Jan. 1944 Anchored Ulithi Lagoon, Caroline Is. ... 1115.0
58- 6 Feb. 1945 Departed Ulithi Lagoon
8 Feb. 1945 Anchored Apra Harbor, Guam 383.0
59- 17 Feb. 1945 Departed Apra Harbor (3rd Mar Div. embarked)
27 Feb. 1945 Anchored at Iwo Jima, Volcanic Is. 2429.0
60- 27 Feb. 1945 to March 5, 1945 Night retirements 401.0
61- 5 Mar. 1945 Departed Iwo Jima
8 Mar. 1945 Anchored Apra Harbor, Guam 750.0

214

62- 9 Mar. 1945 Departed Apra Harbor
     16 Mar. 1945 Anchored Tulagi Harbor, Solomons Is.   <u>1950.0</u>

     Total miles traveled in the Pacific: 49,066

     To Noumea, New Caledonia   Total grand miles: 70,800